D0441497

Relating Psychically:

Psychic Influences on Relationships

Sandra J. Stevens

Cassandra Press
San Rafael, Ca. 94915

Cassandra Press
P.O. Box 868
San Rafael, Ca. 94915

Printed in the United States of America.

First printing 1989.

ISBN 0-945946-01-5

Library of Congress Catalogue Card Number 88-63534

The use of the material described in this text is not meant to replace the services of a physician who should always be consulted for any condition requiring his or her aid.

Front cover art by Susan St. Thomas. Copyright ©1988 Cassandra Press.

Table of Contents

Author's Note..i

Acknowledgment..ii

Chapter I   What are Psychic Influences in Relationships?.................... 1

Chapter II   Families That Reincarnate Together................................. 9

Chapter III   Parents and Children: Who Chooses Whom?......................19

Chapter IV   Children and Parents: Who Affects Whom?.......................27

Chapter V   Children and Parents: Healing Together............................35

Chapter VI   Psychic Bonds..45

Chapter VII   "Haven't We Met Before?" 53

Chapter VIII   "Who Me? Thinking of You?"..61

Chapter IX   Relationships as Learning Grounds: Beliefs......................73

Chapter X   Relationships as Learning Grounds: Patterns....................83

Chapter XI   Relationships as Learning Grounds: HOW WE SET IT UP!.97

Chapter XII   Sex: Doing It? and With Whom? 105

Chapter XIII   Friends, Enemies and Others 119

Chapter XIV   Death as a Psychic Event of Life................................. 131

Chapter XV   Summing Up..147

Author's Note

This book is the result of years of counseling done at Mind Matters, a meta-physical counseling service located in Washington Crossing, Pennsylvania. My partner, trance-channel Sheila Reynolds, and I have conducted thousands of sessions over the past decade, at least 80 percent of which involved relationship issues. As I saw certain patterns emerging in these sessions, as well as in my own life, I realized that, even with the numerous books available on relationships, no one had written a comprehensive book about subtle, psychic influences that affect each of us daily in our own relationships. I also wanted to continue teaching the concepts of metaphysical awareness—that we are all more than we think we are; that is, we are multidimensional beings with many explorations contributing toward our learning. Also, we create our own reality; and to understand this concept, in regard to the others who move through our lives, seemed extremely important to me.

You will notice that I chose to write about myself in the third person, a device I began in my first book, *Being Alive Is Being Psychic*. I find that I can be more comfortably objective about my own learning with the distance this point-of-view affords. All names, except those of my and Sheila's immediate families, have been changed to protect the privacy of our friends and clients. Occasionally, places and factual circumstances have also been changed for the same purpose; however, the essence of the events remains true—as true as is possible from my perspective.

I wish, of course, to thank Sheila Reynolds for her continuing contribution to my life as a friend and supporter, and for the opportunity to know and work with the wisdom of the nonphysical entity who speaks through her, Gay Bonner. I also wish to thank Linda Killian for her conscientious reading and correcting of the manuscript. And to all those friends, visible and invisible, who contribute toward my learning, I send my on-going love.

Sandra J. Stevens

For "Len"

who forced me to learn by

being who he is!

Chapter I

What Are Psychic Influences in Relationships?

On October 22, 1979, the *Philadelphia Bulletin* printed the following article:
ALL'S WELL THAT . . .
A lover's spat back in 1932 over what neither participant can remember ended happily over the weekend in Salt Lake City when John B. Calhoun, 72, and Hazel Biles, 68, were married. Childhood sweethearts back in Guthrie, Okla., the couple broke up and each married another person. Mrs. Biles, a widow who was living in Salem, Ore., recently was contacted by Calhoun, by then divorced. He finally popped the question after six telephone calls.

In January of 1983, a farming couple, who also worked as security guards at the University of Nebraska, underwent multiple by-pass surgery, one day apart. Married 40 years, the wife was operated on January 10th, the husband on January 11th.

"We knew if we didn't have it done, we'd have to live a very limited kind of life. ... we would really have to take it easy, which we just weren't prepared to do," according to the husband. I just said, 'I'll go if you go, and he said that was fine with him,' she reported. (*Philadelphia Inquirer,* January 25, 1983).

COUPLE CLOSE IN LIFE DIE MOMENTS APART (Associated Press)

CHICAGO—Florence Graziano had just visited Salvatore, her husband of 51 years, in his hospital room and had returned to her own room when at the exact minute he was pronounced dead, her heart also stopped.

"He was a sick man, and his death was not a surprise," said Dr. Nancy Streitmatter, a cardiologist at Illinois Masonic Hospital. "But she had a small heart attack with no complications and would have been released soon. Everyone here was stunned."

After 9 a.m. Monday, Mrs. Graziano, 70, was wheeled into her husband's room. She knew he was dying and that she would be saying goodbye. Minutes after she had returned to her room, Mr. Graziano, 79, died and his wife suffered a cardiac arrest.

"She arrested at the exact time that her husband was pronounced dead—at 9:09 a.m., " said Joy Clich, head nurse of the coronary-care unit.

"It was an eerie thing, and nobody on staff can believe it. "

"We try to be scientific as doctors, but we're very human, " said Streitmatter, "And when the son-in-law said to me, 'I think she just couldn't live without him,' I had to say yes."

"They were dependent on each other," said one of their daughters, Judy Hoehler. "My mother didn't drive. My father took her everywhere, and she took care of everything for him. They kept each other young."

"Part of it," explained the oldest daughter, Rosalie Kowalske, "was that their emotions were so tied to each other, even more than any of us knew." (*Philadelphia Inquirer*, 8-3-84).

Sometime in 1982, a sixteen-year-old Down's syndrome boy was operated on to patch a hole between the chambers of his heart. As a result of the operation, the boy would probably have a fuller, longer, and healthier life. The operation, however, was performed only after a five-year legal fight between two couples, both claiming that they desired what was best for the boy. His biological parents were adamantly against the operation, arguing that their son would not improve and was best served in institutions. They expressed concern that he would outlive them and there would be no one to care for him. They had placed him in nurseries and boarding homes immediately after birth. The other couple, once volunteers at a home where he stayed, began taking him home weekends. They "fell in love" (their words) with him ten years before the operation and in 1981, sued to gain custody which was granted and upheld by higher courts. It was this couple, as his legal guardians, that obtained the operation.

TROUBLES STILL FOLLOW MAN AND TEENAGE WIFE (United Press International)

ERIE—A teenager and her former schoolteacher, whose marriage has been held up for two years despite legal attempts to prevent it, are still facing hard times.

The two, whose relationship might prompt a revision of Pennsylvania's marriage laws, celebrated their second anniversary last week. In an interview, they said they were deeply in debt and deeply in love.

The former teacher, Edward Christoph, has not worked since he was fired from a middle school in the Erie area after his common-law marriage to the student, Melissa Miller, in August, 1981. She was 14 at the time; he was 37.

Christoph, an Erie native who was an English teacher with a master's degree in education, is trying to find a teaching position. But for now, the couple is living in a wood frame rowhouse on $132 a month in welfare payments and $126 a month in food stamps. Sharing the house is Christoph's daughter, Kim, 14, from an earlier marriage.

"Our relationship is probably the best it's ever been," he said. "Anyone who went through the hassle and turmoil of the first year of our marriage can handle just about anything that can turn up. The only problem is it's tough to live without any income."

When they first wed as common-law partners, his wife's mother had the marriage annulled. The girl was declared a ward of the court and sent to live with relatives in California. She returned last summer after an appeal, with the court upholding her right to marry at age 14 under the common law.

"I was under a lot of pressure to drop the appeal," said Mrs. Christoph. "My family said if I'd drop it they'd get me a motorcycle."

Now she rides her husband's motorcycle and plays softball on the team he coaches for the Wesleyville Baptist Church.

They went to the church last month and renewed their vows officially because she had reached the legal age of 16 and could wed under civil marriage law.

Mrs. Christoph, who missed a great deal of school last year due to an illness, said she planned to return to high school for her sophomore year in September. (*Philadelphia Inquirer*, 7-28-83).

These are just a few of the numerous stories in the newspapers every week that raise questions, causing us to wonder, scratch our heads, and ask how and why such things happen—that a man or a couple would go to such extreme lengths to break with law and convention to marry a child or save one's life; that "coincidences" can be so strange; or that a couple could reunite after forty-seven years and rekindle a romance?

Are there influences beyond the obvious ones—influences that may even defy our reason, our logic? This book is about just such influences and how they affect us in our relationship to one another.

The intense closeness between Sandy and her oldest son, Steven is often confusing, complicated, and at times, touching. The summer of Steven's fourteenth year, he was away from home for six weeks visiting relatives and camping with his father. About the fifth week, Sandy had a strange adventure. She and Sheila had returned to her house from their Mind Matters' office after a couple of morning sessions with people who had come to talk to Gay Bonner, the spirit guide who had been counseling people through the mediumship of Sheila Reynolds for the past five or so years. The two women had decided to return to Sandy's house for lunch and a private session with Gay for themselves. Sandy arrived first as Sheila stopped at the post office. After driving down her long gravel driveway, Sandy realized that she had not stopped at her mailbox on the road to take in her mail. As she walked back toward the mailbox, she saw a robin sitting in the middle of the driveway. That, of course, was not unusual until she realized that the bird was not flying away as she approached it. She stooped down to take a closer look and saw that the robin was old, or sick. It gazed up at her pathetically. Glancing back over her shoulder, she saw her two big yellow cats sauntering toward her. Concerned for the bird, she gently lifted it, carrying it into the woods where it could die safely. She then went to the mailbox, took out the mail and began walking back just as Sheila drove into the driveway. Sheila got out of her car and started walking down the driveway toward Sandy waving some pages of Mind Matters' mail. Suddenly she stopped and called out, "Look here's a robin, just sitting here."

The bird was back—in the same spot from which Sandy had removed it moments earlier. Amazed, she picked it up again, talking to it gently about dying peacefully instead of violently as the cats tore it apart. She carried it even deeper into the woods and surrounded it with a shelter of sticks and leaves. Overcome with sad yet peaceful feelings, she cried awhile then went back to Sheila and the work at hand.

Later during the session with Gay, she asked about several emotional events in her life during the past week, including her feelings about the bird in the driveway. She was surprised when Gay, speaking through Sheila, said the following:

"That bird out there is an aspect of your child, Steven. He, of course, is not conscious of this but what might be a tiny spark of energy from him created this bird who is now ill. I feel that you needed to express your tenderness to this bird so Steven can feel today some mother love which he wants right now... The bird accepted your love. Steven felt happy. He's missed you but certainly he's much too big to cry or admit it so what you have given to the bird was felt by him. He needed this love which the bird willingly accepted."

Sandy was sitting on the back porch of her house the next week when Steven arrived home. Before she could get out of her chair to walk around to the front of the house, he had barreled through the house at top speed, burst through the door onto the porch, picked her up in his arms (proud of his new growth and strength—he was now bigger than she), swung her around, and cried, "Boy, I missed you! Funny, I don't usually, but I did this time!" She knew it, of course. He simply had confirmed it for her.

Steven has always had an affinity for animals and birds so it was quite natural that he would "work out"—on deep psychic levels—a way of satisfying his needs by sending "a tiny spark of energy from him" to the robin. Not all examples of telepathic communication are so dramatic. In fact, most are rather mundane. The following is a short passage from Sandy's journal, which records a day-to-day incident of telepathy that would normally be easily forgotten by most of us.

"Sheila's and my telepathy has been incredibly sharp lately. She'll say what I've been thinking or vice versa. The most recent example concerned using Jack Rosen as our photographer for the book (*Being Alive Is Being Psychic*). I saw him on the streets of New Hope last Sunday and thought to myself, "Why not ask Jack to take our pictures? I must ask Sheila." I didn't see her, but on Monday she had the thought, "Why not use Jack Rosen for the pictures?"—my exact thought—and called him to set it up, leaving a message on my answering machine to let me know what she'd done!"

The thoughts and feelings of others close to us are strong influences on us as we create our lives. Sometimes thoughts are transmitted directly, as between Sandy and Sheila, and sometimes indirectly, through an event as with Steven's feelings. At other times, the communication occurs in dreams.

Pat had not seen Harold for about a month. As far as she was concerned, the relationship was over and she had begun to date other men. Then she had a dream. In the dream Harold was very sick and close to death. When she was a child, Pat had learned to pay attention to her dreams as they often contained messages that later became true. She called him. He was preparing to go to the hospital for a brain operation. He had a tumor and told her that he had a fifty-fifty chance of survival. For Pat the dream represented proof of a bond between them. She went to him. He survived and they are now married. Harold has never believed her and teases that the "story" of the dream was just an excuse to get back together with him. Pat shrugs and rolls her eyes as she says, "He's so dense! How would I have even known he was sick if not for the dream?"

Pat, because of her experiences, trusts her dreams and the kind of communication that sometimes comes through them. For Harold, it is difficult to understand because he has not experienced such things in a way that he can consciously accept. That, however, does not mean that he is not influenced by such psychic happenings. He is, whether he denies the dream or not, now married to Pat.

Numerous and varied examples of telepathy appear throughout this book. Another psychic influence that will be covered in depth here is "past lives"—explorations in other times and places that are closely connected to who we are now and the learning that we have chosen for this particular time/space reality. Once we open to the validity of such explorations, we find that we can "understand" situations in our lives that may otherwise be mystifying.

Sandy found herself in an amusing series of encounters that hinted to her of these other realities. Several years ago, while still selling pharmaceuticals, she called on a particular mental health treatment center. She had easy rapport with the psychiatrists there and usually enjoyed stopping by. One secretary, however, always treated her as if she were an intruder, maybe even dangerous. The behavior was consistent for the year or so that she frequented the center. At first she thought that perhaps the secretary had a "special" relationship with one of the doctors or that she felt that it was her duty to "protect" the doctors from outsiders, especially strange women. As time went on, however, the doctors changed, the rest of the staff was open and cordial to Sandy's presence, and the secretary remained hostile. One day, leaving the center after a particularly uncomfortable encounter, Sandy shrugged, laughing to herself, "I must have done something terrible to her in a past life!"

On her next visit the secretary was gone and Sandy soon forgot all about her. Four years later she walked into an office in another part of town. She was there to elicit some specific marketing information for her sales manager. The receptionist behind the desk seemed familiar but Sandy did not remember where they might have met. She gave the woman her card and told her why she was there. She had simple, superficial questions to ask, and had successfully and easily done so at many other offices. The woman immediately balked and began to argue with her, insisting that she felt very uncomfortable talking to her. "But what I'm asking for is not confidential," Sandy countered. The woman repeated that she felt "uncomfortable" talking to her. Sandy then remembered who she was and asked her if she had worked at the mental health center that she had once called on. The woman's face lit up, then frowned, as she recalled, "Yes, I do remember you now. I thought you looked familiar."

Sandy, much to the woman's surprise, began to laugh: "Look, it's okay. You didn't like me then so it's not surprising that you feel the same way now. I don't take it personally."

The woman was abashed and protested, "But it's not you. I don't even really know you."

"Yes, yes, I know. Don't worry. Perhaps I remind you of an obnoxious great aunt or something. Really, I don't take it personally."

Perhaps it was a great aunt—in this lifetime or in another. It doesn't really matter in this situation what the influence is. What is important is recognizing that there is an influence involved, accepting it, and, for Sandy, realizing that she does not need to take the woman's behavior toward her personally. Strong feelings that arise when we meet people that are out of proportion to the present situation are indications that there is more going on than is obvious. Staying open to possibilities can be both fun and freeing.

Deborah had recently married for the second time. She desperately wanted the marriage to work. In this relationship, as in others before it, she found herself repeating a familiar pattern. Always in the beginning, Deborah would feel strong and independent, but as time went by, she would begin to feel powerless and insignificant. Her response to this feeling would be to begin pushing at her lover or mate, trying to obtain some sign or proof that she belonged. In every instance, the feelings of powerlessness arose from a sense of not belonging, of being separate from those around her. She came to Sandy for therapy to help her marriage, and in the course of the therapy, had a session with Sheila to talk to Gay:

"You ask about feeling separate, feeling not connected. What is happening here is that you are actually very connected at inner levels—at the psychic level you are very connected. You are feeling what is happening at this deep reality and I feel that you have often been with someone who also feels not connected and psychically you pick that up and it intensifies your own feelings of separateness and aloneness. I am not certain that you were so wanted at birth in this present lifetime, and I feel here some trauma at birth that intensifies the feeling of separateness. I feel some physical birth trauma here. Difficulty with being able to breathe, cut off from the supply of air, and I feel this greatly influences this reaction that you carry with you.

"There is also trauma in dying in another lifetime where you were choking to death and could not breathe. I see here that you were choked to death by someone else—a lover. This was in the last century in France. You were quarreling and I see someone choking you to death, someone who was very jealous. Now I feel, of course, memories of this carried into this present existence and you need to feel at times separate in order to feel safe. The history of that relationship in that other life was one of constant danger and violence. Now I feel that the man in that lifetime has been with you in this life but is no longer around you, and now you need to concentrate on letting go of that in order to be in the present reality."

Her own psychic sensitivity, birth trauma, and a past life—all influence her feelings and her behavior in her present reality. This book will illustrate how such influences reflect and affect the patterns in our lives and the personal and cultural beliefs that underlie them, creating the reality that we live.

8 Relating Psychically

Chapter II

Families that Reincarnate Together

"You've got to be kidding! I would never *choose* to be in that family!"

"Of course! It makes perfect sense that my family and I have come together to give each other support."

"I don't know about that! The idea that I might have chosen to throw myself into that den of lions is intriguing, but why would I do such a stupid thing?"

These are just a few of the responses people give the first time they hear the idea that they may have deliberately *chosen* the families in which they are stuck—crazy old Aunt Susie, that snooty older cousin, the judgmental, cranky grandfather, as well as mother, father, sister, brother, daughter, and son. Joyfully or reluctantly, we have to admit that we do have some say when it comes to husbands and wives; however, blood relatives are different. Why would we deliberately choose most of them?

Back in 1978, during the first years of Sheila and Sandy's work with Mind Matters and Gay Bonner, they decided to experiment with "life readings," similar to those Edgar Cayce had done for people's children. They suspected that sessions for children would deal mostly in probabilities as yet not physically realized but nonetheless influenced by past life experiences, by beliefs carried into current reality, and by choices made for future learning during this lifetime. To begin this experiment, they used Sandy's children as subjects.

"Griffin is in this family to be exposed to and learn spiritual matters. He did live in the time of Christ but mostly has always been concerned with physical matters—survival and nature. He has spent lives where he fished and hunted. These are interests he may turn to later. His interests in life may be very different from yours (Sandy's) but he needs to learn yours too. He chose his father because of similar interests, particularly in dogs. He also has affinity for dogs. Your relationship with him will be one of some lack of understanding on both sides."

Earlier in the session, Gay had said that Griffin, Sandy's youngest son, who was seven years old at the time of this reading, had come into this life in order to rest after many lifetimes of struggle on the physical plane—in Alaska and in the wilds of Siberia, where each day was filled with striving for food and warmth.

She also described Griffin's life during the time of Christ where he knew his father and his older brother, Steven:

"He (Griffin's father, Bill) and Steven were his friends during the time of Christ. All were fishermen. Steven went to travel with a very large group of Christians and tried to get his friends to come but did not succeed. Bill and Griffin both preferred fishing."

So, Gay went on to explain, Griffin was attracted to this particular family to learn of spiritual matters, to rest from struggles on the physical plane, and to be with his father and brother. At this writing, Griffin is fourteen years old. Sandy has witnessed a lack of understanding between herself and this youngest son, whom she had not known before. However, armed with the knowledge given to her in this session, she has been able to step back emotionally when needed and allow this child the learning he has chosen for himself. Griffin has been exposed to spiritual thought and experience as a result of choosing to be with this family—particularly his mother and brother, with their spiritual orientation. He also has had an important ally in his father with whom he hunts, fishes, and raises dogs—all interests that have developed naturally as he's grown older.

The differences in Sandy's interactions with her two sons were a puzzle to her for many years. Somehow, even though Griffin seems to struggle more in his life than Steven does, Sandy usually feels clear while parenting Griffin, able to be in the role of mother with relative ease and confidence. With Steven that was not the case. Right from the birth of her older son, Sandy often felt confused and "upside down" while relating to him. The emotional intensity between them would rise and fall like the waves in a storming ocean. With Griffin, she would often feel clear currents of unconditional love no matter what would be happening on the physical plane. With Steven, the love she felt was often clouded with expectations, with confusion as to its nature, with anger, with judgment from her to him and him to her, with an awe for his innate "knowing" about things little kids don't normally know—a myriad of constantly shifting feelings and perceptions.

Steven was eleven years old when Sheila and Sandy did their life reading on him. Gay talked of a life of preparation for some work he has chosen to do someday:

"There seems to be a strong probability he will not know definitely what he wants to do until late in life. To others this will seem like indecision and floundering. It will be more to the point to say that he will be learning and studying and perceiving for major work that will be done late in life—later than you (Sandy) will want.

"In order to do what I feel he has "planned," it takes long preparation in dreaming and living. You, Sandy, need to let go of your expectations, for he and you were friends in Atlantis. He was a teacher of yours. He was also a friend, but he kept pushing at you to write. You resisted his pushing. He saw what you could do but, like he is now you were then, and needed time. He is here now also to show you how relative time is. There is plenty of time. He will prove this to you. You will be letting go of your expectations as you give yourself time."

Time is perhaps Sandy's biggest issue in her present lifetime. She struggles with time as other people struggle with money, sex, or parents. Steven moves at his own pace. He is now eighteen and this struggle continues between them, Sandy constantly pushing, Steven resisting in a quiet, passive way. The learning is slow—but perhaps that too is appropriate!

The information that Steven had once been a teacher to Sandy was very helpful to her in explaining some of the feelings and confusing behaviors that would occur between them. That wasn't the end of the explanation, however. Gay went on to say that they had shared many, many lifetimes, playing out almost every possible relationship—friends, lovers, spouses. Steven had been her father and her guide. Never before had they been mother and son. Hearing that explained much of the difficulty Sandy experienced when trying to be in the role of mother to him. This was new and they were trying it out. Knowing that finally made it possible for Sandy to step back and simply laugh when Steven would behave like a jealous lover or a bossy father. She also learned to accept his wisdom with grace instead of resentment, realizing that he had once been her teacher and even her guide. Gay stressed the multitude of different connections between them and the strength of their psychic bond. The struggles of their early years together eased as Steven moved into adolescence, and those possibly difficult years flowed by, filled with love, fun, and an intimacy that Sandy continues to treasure. Relating to time remains the biggest challenge between them!

Griffin chose his family to be with his father and brother, introducing himself to his mother for the first time. Steven, although he knew his brother and father, seems to have been primarily tied to Sandy.

Sometimes families reincarnate as a group. One family that Sheila and Sandy have worked with over the years share a particular intimacy and history that seems to have pulled them all together in this particular time/space exploration. The Emerson family consists of a mother with four children, three sons and one daughter. The father died fifteen years ago. The mother and daughter share the same first name, Barbara. All except one son have had sessions with Gay and all have asked about their connections with one another. The ties are complicated and challenging but the main components of this family relationship are support and love.

The daughter was the first family member to talk to Gay:

"I see a life that is influencing you now. A life where you had a marriage and a close family. Your brothers now were your children in this life and I see there was much happiness for you. You might think that this would be cause for joy now but quite the opposite. I feel at a deeper level you could not believe you deserved to have such peace and you wondered when it would end. You could not accept a restful, peaceful life and so it (the "not accepting") continues now."

At a later point, Gay said, "I feel you and your mother have been sisters many times. There is a close psychic connection here and you often have telepathic contact. Even without realizing it, you send thoughts back and forth."

To one of her brothers, Gay said, "I have referred in your sister's session to a tie with her where she was your mother. I also see your mother now as a mother many times so there is a kind of comfortable rapport here."

A second brother was given a deeper explanation for his involvement with this family—one not unlike Griffin's:

"This particular lifetime for you is a lesson in introspection and spiritual realization. This is why you "chose" the family that you have. Part of their function has been to help you see life's deeper messages and meaning. Although not outwardly "spiritual," I feel the potential in your family and the connection for you has been to have their acceptance and to allow them to lead you to these "New Age" concepts. I see you with many, many lifetimes, many of a very superficial nature, and many times you died quickly and violently, and often in shock, immediately focusing your consciousness into another lifetime, quickly entering the physical body of an infant often without adequate thought and preparation.

"You have, in many lifetimes, been without focus and often disoriented. You needed your family to provide you with a safe basis and some comfort from many shocks in other lifetimes. You often lived lives where you felt unprotected. Often you lived without family ties and connections. You were with this particular family of your present existence in the Far East, and you had much of the same closeness that you have now. After many, many lifetimes you needed to be reunited."

The mother's information on her connection with her children also involved some "karma" with her own parents:

"It was not easy for you with your parents. I sense that they were both very distant and cold, very stern and "moral." You must give yourself credit for all you have accomplished. You must realize your own ability to love others. This you have doubted, but your children were drawn to you so that you could see within yourself your ability to love others. That is why Barbara and David are with you. They are like teachers to you. Barbara has given you much in terms of learning about the spiritual aspects of reality and David has opened you to your feelings. They have shown you that you can love and that you are beautiful, despite what kind of feedback you received from your parents."

In another session, Gay talked about Barbara's youngest son:

"You already are aware that you and Paul have been together many times. He has been your father many times and because of your relationship with your father now, you have turned to Paul for support. I feel that he was very close in many other lives. I see an existence in Austria where he was your father. You were a man and you both went into business together. I feel that you needed to have Paul's support in this lifetime and that you need to simply allow this to exist and permit yourself to receive as much as you can here. He gives quite freely to you. You are both, however, receiving much from this relationship. Do not feel guilty. You realize, of course, you do much for Paul also."

About three years after receiving this information from Gay, Barbara Emerson underwent some dramatic psychic events that pulled together, not only the issue of her relationship to her parents, but also the learning Gay referred to concerning the acceptance of support. Barbara had always been the strong "matriarch" of her family, doing for others, supporting them emotionally, worrying about them, taking care of them in the way she believed mothers should. In February, 1985, she received a healing from an Indian healer with whom she wanted to train. This session intensified some physical symptoms that became so severe she could not work. She saw medical doctors who could find no apparent physical cause for the symptoms. She knew she needed to resolve the underlying psychic causes of these symptoms in order to go on with her life, and she wanted to come from the Midwest to Pennsylvania to work with Sandy and Sheila. However, she was broke. Unable to work for months, she had been forced to receive help from her son, David. This made her extremely uncomfortable. When everything intensified; David, Paul and daughter Barbara, insisted that she come and allow them to assist her in doing so. Young Barbara offered to pay for the sessions. David continued to pay her living expenses, and Paul paid for the gas needed to drive to Pennsylvania. Barbara was learning an intense lesson in receiving from her own children.

Much of the work accomplished during the two days of sessions with Sheila and Sandy involved the relationship with her parents. The physical symptoms she had been experiencing were in part due to the harshness of that relationship and her subsequent anger at her parents, particularly her father. She had been an only child and was expected to care for them whenever they desired it, but was given little in return. Her father had led her to believe that they had been very poor all of her life. When he died she found that there had always been money, but that it was lost through bad investments he made just before his death. It was as if he was making sure that she would have nothing from him.

One of the physical symptoms that had intensified and brought her to Sandy's office was excessive mucus in her chest, often reaching a point where she could not breathe. This mucus was not infected and seemed to have no medical cause. Gay had referred to this symptom three years earlier:

"It is through opening your heart on a psychic level that the mucus can begin to dissolve. I see you giving forth much energy and love but being reluctant to receive for yourself. This is also what stops you from having the kind of financial abundance you deserve. You already know that it has much to do with your father. ... It has always been difficult for your father to open his heart to give and so you grew up believing you did not deserve to receive. Asking for what you want was difficult enough, but then you ended up feeling guilty for simply asking. You need to recognize that your father has difficulty in letting go. He needs to be in control, and you have interpreted this as not deserving for yourself. I feel that you have perhaps given too much, always hoping to receive something from him, but it does not come. Of course, at a deep level you want his love and approval. Giving yourself financial abundance means giving up hope of receiving from him and so you remain still a young child, still feeling powerless. You deserve to have money and with it, power, but beyond that is not wanting to totally let go of your father, although of course you never really had him. It is letting go of the hope that you will receive from him."

Three years later, shortly after her father's death, Barbara Emerson sat in Sandy's office talking about her feelings toward her father for never giving her any financial support. She described how angry he was when it became physically impossible for him to handle his finances and Barbara had to take over. She recalled past life information from Gay concerning her parents' anger. She had once, in another time/space exploration, run away from them to become involved with street life and crime. They found out and were furious. Another time in 18th Century England she, as a young boy, was responsible for a fire that took their lives. All of this led to anger and distrust on their part and feelings of guilt and frustration for Barbara, who tried hard to please them over the years with no success. Gay succinctly described the situation:

"I feel that in the relationship with your parents you went to a great deal of effort to please them and to take care of them. Your father in particular was very difficult to please. You tried very hard. You were, in fact, very good to them in your present life but at deeper levels it was thought never to be enough—both by them and by you. There seemed to be no way out, for they could not show any appreciation. It seemed to be very difficult, but perhaps it might be helpful if you can understand the influence of other lives."

Sandy decided that a psychic separation procedure would help. This exercise is designed to help individuals gain some psychic distance and clarity in their relationships with others. It is most helpful in bringing some understanding to the way in which they relate, often helping people let go of influences that are not of the moment so that the present interaction is clear and focused.

Barbara was sitting across from her in a light trance, and Sandy watched her closely for physiological changes that might indicate distress or breakthroughs. When she reached the solar plexus, the part of the exercise having to do with power—that is, who is in control of the relationship—Barbara's breathing became labored. She gasped for breath, pulled her legs up to her chest, held on to her stomach, and began an inarticulate moan. She reported no images or cognitive sense of what was happening, simply tremendous physical and emotional feeling. Sandy quickly laid her down and urged her to "enter into the feeling." Still no visual or cognitive input. Barbara said she only felt nauseated. Sandy grabbed a wastebasket and told her to throw up. She resisted at first but Sandy kept assuring her that it was okay, that she was not bad for wanting to throw it all up.

Finally she did. Sitting with Sandy's hand on her back, she discharged loads and loads of grey matter. There was no food, simply mucus. All her repressed anger, all the years of trying so hard, all the resentment for not being able to make them give to her, the feeling of imprisonment because she still lived in and cared for their house and not her own, came up into that wastebasket. Barbara Emerson was exhausted, but relieved. Sandy remembered the same feeling from her own therapy years before when she too had thrown up similar feelings into a wastebasket.

Barbara was not finished there, however. She talked to Gay once again. Gay told her of a lifetime in Ireland during a potato famine. She had had many children, including those from this present lifetime. Most of them died and she could do nothing to save them. Barbara had always had a strong aversion to visiting England or Ireland even though she loved to travel. Gay told her that examining this Irish lifetime would answer many of her questions.

The second major symptom Barbara brought to Sandy and Sheila was a sensation of a tremendous weight on her chest that would lead to a feeling that she must pull up her legs and push—as if giving birth—in order to relieve the pressure. This physical reaction would come over her and she seemingly had no choice but to experience the pain and pressure of birthing, along with an emotional sadness that felt like loss. This symptom appeared during the hypnosis session Sandy was conducting to examine the Irish lifetime. The kinesthetic feelings were so overpowering that Barbara was unable to move beyond them and "know" what was causing them. Sandy insisted that she say "NO" to the feelings. Saying "no" had been an important part of all her sessions because of her extreme need to do for others, to please others. Finally Barbara was able to communicate with the woman she once was in Ireland. The most important part of that communication was to assure that "other" self (her past-life self in Ireland) that she had survived and so had her children. Barbara telepathically gave this assurance over and over until she finally gained the attention of her other self and her present self calmed down.

Many issues fell into place. Barbara realized how important it was to allow her children to give to her, breaking a cycle of many lifetimes. She realized that she could love them and still let go of them, knowing they would be safe. She recognized that it was time to let go of her parents, her guilt, and go on with her own life. She had done everything she possibly could.

The closeness of Barbara Emerson's present family made it possible for her to work out lifetimes of karma and karmic patterns. The support and love of her children gave her the resources she needed to complete an important piece of growth work. Certainly others choose families for the same purpose. Griffin has done so. Al Teamer did the same.

The gentle, late-middle-aged man sat quietly in front of Sandy and Sheila talking about himself. He had come to ask about a relationship with a woman who had just left him to marry a "macho" man who ordered her about. Al couldn't understand why. As he talked, he seemed to swing between two very different ways of being in the world. One moment he was rational, logical, and "objective." He was, after all, a scientist, an astronomer by profession. The next moment, he would be a feeling, emotional human, unable to understand how he got himself into this painful spot. He had had two marriages. His first wife was killed in a plane crash. He had been the pilot. The second had a brain tumor that made her crazy. After years of suffering, he finally left her.

Al had been drawn to his family by his father, Gay reported. His father had "called out" for him. She went on:

"I feel also that you needed to have the struggles that you have had to learn of your strength. You have been fighting for your life since before birth and in many other lifetimes. Even the birth itself was a difficult process for you resisted and I feel you fought to stay where you were, and I see you fighting even as a child. You had to be strong. ... I feel that throughout your life, despite the friendships you enjoyed, there is a basic sense of loneliness and separateness that you carry with you, a part of you that you cannot show in your relationships, for you spend much of your time taking care of others.

"I see you in another existence that has colored this existence in regards to having to be strong for others. You were a military leader, one that cared deeply about the men you were charged with. And I see that despite fear and even great physical pain, you did not break down or lose control of your emotions. You were rewarded for this kind of behavior by the men you served, and I feel that you believed this was how you had to be. Of course, this is but one influence. There are many in your life. At the opposite extreme is a life where you practiced healing arts, and you were very open to the emotions of others. You were a woman, and I feel that there is conflict between these two aspects of yourself. One says you must be a certain way for this is what it means to be a man. The other says that to be alive is to feel and be open. *As you can see, your parents represent two aspects of yourself that were in conflict, so your parents enacted a drama that goes on and has gone on inside of you.* I feel that you came here tonight because you are ready to let go of many old influences and to be at peace, to allow yourself to stop fighting."

Gay went on to talk about his present relationship but the main thrust of his session was to emphasize the struggles in his life that had come out of his own inner conflict. Sandy was curious about Al's parents and asked if his father was strong and masculine with definite ideas about how a man should be.

"No," Al replied. "In fact, it was just the opposite. My mother was angry and harsh. She didn't want me and, at birth, I almost died. She was always cold to me and my father. He was an artist and very passive."

Sandy and Sheila were surprised. Al's conflict, "enacted" by his parents, and reflected by his own shifting personality, took an unconventional twist—the woman he'd once been was now being acted out by his father. The masculine characteristics were now embodied in his mother. Gay also had talked about the creative energy he would release as he lets go of these influences.

Gay emphasizes the "choice" we make each time we enter into physical life and into a particular family. Talking to the mother of a pre-adolescent boy who had been quite ill, she ties together his responsibility in choosing this family as well as the karmic patterns they all have chosen to work out.

"You are not responsible for the overall choices that your children make, for they also chose to be born and then chose this specific family for their own learning purposes. ... Even in lives other than this life, Tommy has been your son. I see several other lives where he has been your son but you are not responsible for his lack of will to live. There are other influences operating here. I feel that Cathy (his older sister) is an influence here. She and Tommy have been together before and I see that they were once brothers who were fighting in a civil war in Spain. I see that they were on different sides and Tommy killed Cathy. I see that resentment here even at his birth. I also feel that his attachment to you was what brought him to this family. Although he has been with his father before it was very briefly. His father was the headmaster of a boy's school in London where Tommy was and Tommy did very poorly here. I feel that there is not the closeness that Tommy needs from his father but you must remember that he also chose this."

This mother had recently been making decisions about what she wanted in her own life. Gay describes how that process was affecting the entire family:

"I see that your decision about taking care of yourself and taking charge of your own life makes a big difference to your children for they often act out the feelings for the entire family—the feelings particularly that your husband is unable to express. Your relationship with your husband has been mirrored in your children's behavior. The relationship between Cathy and Tommy is a similar struggle to that between you and your husband—only theirs is an outward manifestation. ... Do what you want to do and their behavior will change. If you are clear and happier, they will be also."

Decisions as to which family to join, then, can be based on several influences. Sometimes those influences are from past life experience, sometimes to work out karmic patterns—that is, to take advantage of "learning" opportunities. Sheila and Sandy had wondered why they had chosen their particular families and had often remarked how similar their relationships to their families were. They occasionally lamented their lack of involvement with their parents and siblings. Their perspective on that changed, however, when Gay told them that they had deliberately chosen their families in order to be free to develop their work in this life. To Sheila she said, "You need a family like yours so you can do the work there is to be done. They don't make demands on you emotionally. You still have feelings around them but basically they make few demands of time or energy." To Sandy she said, "You have the same opportunity Sheila does to be able to work independently with little interference."

Sometimes the feeling of non-involvement or being on the "outside" brings with it a different message or different learning. One woman to whom Gay spoke had been struggling with the anger and pain of not being wanted by her parents:

"I feel that you were not welcome when conceived and your soul felt this very deeply. I feel your parents made some adjustments but hoped for a son, and here too, you, in this sense, disappointed them. Your subconscious carries with you this deep feeling of not belonging, and I feel it is no wonder that you feel alienated from these people. Do not blame yourself for this feeling of being alienated, for they are a part of this distance. There is not true warmth coming from them and so to protect yourself you have created distance here. I see that these parents were children to you in another life and you were very poor and as a result could not care for them. You put them in a home but not without a great deal of guilt and that guilt drew you to them in this life and made you experience what you did. You can see for yourself other effects from that lifetime. You need only remember your own childhood and you can see the connections."

Another kind of influence came up in this same session. Gay later went on to say that her parents also exerted a "psychic influence. Your mother does not want you to be any happier than she could ever be and this is the psychic message she sends to you."

This sort of telepathic "message" is not uncommon in family relationships. To a young man who was just beginning to assert himself in the world, Gay said:

"I see you letting go of old concepts and ideas about who you are and so the distance from your parents is a very good thing for now.

"Your mother was comfortable as long as you were like you used to be. You need to believe that in time you can be truly close. I do not feel that you ever were as close as you thought. The outward motions exist but only as long as you remained a good boy. They are sending you psychic messages to go back to being a good boy even though when you were their good boy, you kept much of what you thought undesirable hidden from them. Now there is nothing to hide but they are not so pleased. Strange, isn't it? But again simply a lesson. They are people with their own individual realities as well as being your parents."

Another even subtler telepathic influence occurred when one woman who came to talk to Gay was planning to leave her marriage. She wanted desperately to be away from her husband but "something" held her there. Gay explained, "There is a child involved in the pull toward your husband. I feel there is a child who does desire to have you both together—the quietest child and seemingly the easiest one to be with. This child needs to let go of old feelings. You are very affected by this child for you want to make this child happy. I feel that there is a deeper level of communication happening here, and the child constantly thinking of you both together causes you to be influenced and still feel as though you cannot let go."

Awareness of all the ways in which we interact with our family members can bring to us opportunities to learn, an understanding of complex feelings and dynamics, and a sense of the rich and creative multidimensional nature of our relationships.

Chapter III

Parents and Children:
Who Chooses Whom?

"Most of the world would believe me crazy," Sandy thought. For days she had been entering a meditative state and "arguing" with a female entity who wanted her to do something she did not want to do. It started with the usual symptoms—bloating, burping, swollen breasts, weight gain, then nausea, lightheadedness, and a sense of "undefined" physical boundaries. She knew what she had to do. These symptoms had appeared three or four times over the past five years or so. Each time she sensed the same entity around her, demanding to be born. Each time, Sandy explained that it was not the right time, that she could not allow it, and if it did not agree to leave, then she would be forced to do something she did not want to do and have it violently sucked out. Each time, the entity would finally back off, Sandy would visualize the blood flowing and the event would be finished. This time the entity was insisting that she tell her lover that she was pregnant. "I'm doing that," she would think. "It's my wishful thinking. I just want him to take care of me." She also knew that if she told him, the consequences would be complicated and she could be caught in a web of circumstances that she really wanted to avoid. Each time she meditated, however, the message was the same. "Tell him," the female presence would argue. She got sicker and sicker and the days passed. She thought she might tell him, but given the opportunity, she backed off. She talked to Gay about what was happening:

"There is a spirit who wants you and Len together, believing perhaps this is the way. Your own ambivalence is there. You have been clear about what you have wanted but now a part of you wants to be taken care of and shown some concern and some love. You still do want something from Len. Of course, you are ambivalent about a pregnancy. ... You have drawn to you a persistent, stubborn spirit. Len also plays his part, much more unconsciously than you but this spirit has been his daughter in many lifetimes. ... She has also been a child to you and Len in another life. As you already know, he is torn between wanting to be free but not knowing how this is possible and wanting more of a family."

Sandy admitted her own ambivalence and her need to make her lover give her "concern and some love." She meditated again. This time she felt better about "arguing" with the entity which still insisted that she tell him. Sandy knew though that she was not going to do that nor was she going to have a child at this point in her life. She cut the psychic bonds with the entity and determinedly visualized the blood flowing from her uterus. That night she dreamed about a couple who had lost a child, a girl about three or four years old. Sandy was comforting the father. In the dream she could see the child as a teasing little ghost who kept running around just out of her father's sight. She woke up crying.

Two days later, after seeing her lover and not telling him, she meditated again. The entity was angry. "Why didn't you tell him?" she yelled. (At this point, Sandy was aware that "she" was herself, Sandy, as well as another energy that was very real and part of her and her lover. She found herself thinking that all her "rational" friends would call her crazy, but she knew that what was happening was valid. It simply pushed beyond conventional lines of "reality.") The answer to the question rose up in her like an emotional wave. "I don't trust him." She didn't and so the battle continued. She took steps on the physical plane and got the name of a clinic that performs abortions. That night she gave a party for Sheila's birthday. During the party, her period started with a flood of blood and relief.

The following year, Sandy experienced two similar situations, one right after the other. During the first "pregnancy" in August of that year, she was twelve days late for her period and had all of the accompanying symptoms described above. Again, she had a strong desire to tell her lover, and again she felt the female entity around her. Gay confirmed this for her a second time. She went through a similar process, that time taking the action of buying a pregnancy test. The actions on the physical plane seemed to be the final "cut" which would then bring about her period. She began to have thoughts that she may be in menopause even though she was still young for that. She decided to tell her lover after it was over. When she did, she had her suspicions confirmed. He immediately remarked, "It's a shame that you did not get a chance to use the pregnancy test!"

Sandy thought that was an odd reply and challenged him but he drew back and said, "You are either pregnant or you're not." They did discuss hypothetically the possibility of having a child and he seemed to feel that it was a good idea. It was not for her. She was at a point in her life where her own children were teenagers and she was at last free to pursue a new career of writing and counseling. She realized that this was why she had not trusted him.

Three months later, her period was a couple of weeks late again. This time she had no symptoms. She assumed it was menopause and made an appointment with her doctor for a check-up and the possible use of hormones. Two hours after making that appointment, her period started. Its intensity surprised her and she felt the need to check. She found an embryo. She was shocked because she had had none of the usual symptoms, nor did she psychically experience an entity around her. A week later her gynecologist confirmed that she had been pregnant. She certainly was not menopausal, he insisted. Again she told her lover. She talked to him about her need to know that she could still have children even though she was approaching menopausal age. He responded, "You're telling me I can still have children," as if he had not heard anything she had said about her own motives. That was the last of such events. She did ask Gay why she had not experienced the usual pregnancy symptoms and was told that she needed physical confirmation of the events in order to have "proof" of what had been happening psychically. Both Sandy and her lover had worked through some learning of their own which reflected their ambivalence toward each other and having a child together, and their individual desires to know that they could still have children. The entity has now "given up"—on this lifetime anyway!

As indicated by Sandy's experience, the decision to have children or not is often complicated and deeper than we normally think. In addition to the usual considerations—economics, careers, age, conscious mutual desire, timing, and so on—there are usually deeper psychological and psychic influences which affect the decision making. Past life influences and telepathic messages often play a part even though most of us are not consciously aware of their effects. Two women came to speak to Gay Bonner about the issue of having children. The first was a young woman in her mid-twenties who was absolutely sure she wanted children. So was her husband. She had been unable to get pregnant in spite of numerous medical tests which indicated that she and her husband were both physiologically capable of creating a child. Several influences were affecting her decision:

"I see a life with many children. You were in poverty and you did not want so many children. There was guilt because you felt unable to love these children. You lived in Ireland in a time of famine. The condition of poverty also has influenced your present life. I feel the desire to be secure and safe before having a child. You are safe in your present reality but I still feel the feelings from another existence. ...

"Your husband has been your child before and I feel his resistance to having a child despite what he is conscious of. You are in a sense pleasing him. I feel a closing up inside of you and this is a part of pleasing him. ... There is also a fear of not having a perfect child for in another life I see a child who was mentally retarded. ... Mentally see the body opening and trusting, but realize also that you may not want a child now."

As was often the case, Sandy and Sheila did not see or hear from this young woman for many years. During the writing of these pages, she happened to call the Mind Matters' office for information about classes. Sandy answered the phone that evening and, remembering her name and story because of her work on the book, told her about using her story. The woman excitedly began talking about the effects of this session some eight years ago. "You can't know what that did for me," she exclaimed. "I learned from that session that I had a choice about having children or not and that my body was telling me that I did not want to bear children. I subsequently went through some therapy programs and got in touch with memories from this lifetime. I was present at my sister's birth because my mother couldn't get to the hospital in time. It traumatized me. Knowing that and the information that Gay had given me about Ireland and having had so many children, I knew that I did not want to bear a child. I did want children, however, so four years ago my husband and I adopted a little girl who is the delight of my life. I will always be grateful for that session and the 'permission' not to have a child."

The second woman was also sure that she wanted a child. She felt pushed by her own biological clock. In her late thirties, she was married to a man ten years older than she who had three, college-aged children of his own. He and their mother had divorced when they were quite young and he had suffered much unhappiness during their upbringing. He did not want more children. Gay addressed their struggle:

"It is a very painful area for you both. I feel he is ambivalent about this issue and does not want to admit to feeling that he might want this [having children] again, that he might enjoy this again for the fear is too great that it would be taken away. Now let's focus on you for a moment. Recognize that you have ambivalence also in this area and you are able to both play the opposite side without having to look at the pain involved in the other part of this. You do in a very real sense want to have a child; however, I feel that you have in other lifetimes been very burdened by children. I see a life of constant pregnancies; your husband dying early in his life and you left to care for ten children alone, resenting this a great deal. I also see that you have had malformed children several times and this has influenced your present life.

"Consciously you want to have children, but subconsciously it has been painful to be with children. *Recognize that the conflict is within you, not necessarily between you and your husband, although this is where the drama is acted out.* As you see, he has had pain in being separated from his children. You have had pain being with your children and yet you both have taken a particular side here, not recognizing a deeper ambivalence within you both."

Sometimes entities want to be born so badly they overcome all obstacles on the physical plane. Sandy has a friend who was incarcerated for many years. During his prison stay, he met a woman with two young children and married her. Of course, he was unable to consummate the marriage because of his situation, but their love was strong and she agreed to the marriage and to wait for his release. That release was many years away. Children were quite out of the question. She already had two of her own to raise. Then his brother died. The prison officials let him attend the funeral. The guard accompanying him was sympathetic to his marital situation and allowed him and his wife an hour alone together. Since the intimacy was unexpected, no birth control precautions were taken. They were not concerned about this, however, since it was only once and not a crucial time during her monthly cycle. Nine months later a determined, nine-pound baby boy was born!

Gay has often spoken of entities who wanted to be born to certain couples or individuals. Often she would describe the energy of these entities and their attachments to their potential parents. As in Sandy's case, often their timing is inappropriate. Sometimes not, however, and if not, great obstacles are often overcome in order to bring about the coming together of parents and potential children. Barbara's situation illustrates the complex interaction between the psychic and physical planes to bring about such mergings.

Sandy and Sheila read about Barbara's motherhood in the newspaper. A woman adopted a child in an "open adoption" situation that was unusual in that the adopting parents met the birth mother before the birth, then paced in the father's waiting room of the hospital, awaiting the birth of their son. In the newspaper article, Barbara talked about the emotional complexity of this unusual situation: 'The staff didn't know what to do with us,' giggled the brown-haired woman. ... 'That day was really kind of hard on everybody.' 'It was bizarre,' said Barbara, an easy-going, articulate woman. 'We felt like interlopers, yet we felt we ought to be there. We felt guilty that we were taking somebody else's baby, yet excited that we were having one. Every aspect of it was bittersweet' (*The Philadelphia Inquirer*, 7-6-86). Barbara also reported feeling a bond to the birthing mother. 'Actually, we felt so close to the mother that we wanted to adopt her,' recalled Barbara with a fond smile. 'She was so young herself, and very small and slight. I felt such a bonding toward her that when we left the hospital with the baby, it really hurt me to leave her.' The article also reported that Barbara had conceived herself around the time of her adopted son's birth and was at that time four months pregnant.

Sandy had been moved by the newspaper article and speculated about the interesting possibilities from a psychic perspective. She forgot about it, however, until she received a call from Sheila. Sheila recognized Barbara as a participant of Mind Matters' activities. In fact, a year or so before, she had had a session with Gay Bonner. Sheila told Sandy that Barbara was even doing some of her own psychic channeling. Sandy then realized that this woman had attended one of her workshops the previous August. She decided to call her.

Barbara had been trying to become pregnant for the past five years. She had been through the medical mill—various doctors, tests, drugs—all in vain. She had two letters from specialists in fertility who told her that she could not conceive. For the past two years, however, she had been in contact with two entities who insisted that they would be her children. These contacts came in her own meditations and through various psychics and psychic friends who could feel their presence around Barbara. The entities would indicate that they may not come from natural channels but that they would soon arrive in physical reality. Barbara wondered during this time whether her own wishful dreaming was creating these messages. There were two psychic events in her life, however, which later seemed preparatory to what happened.

The first was a crystal healing that she underwent about a year and a half ago. During that healing she felt a strange flow of energy moving through her body, then became conscious of a lump in the right lower quadrant of her physical body. The energy then began to flow up and up. She started crying over what seemed like nothing. Then she began to laugh, again seemingly over nothing.

Several of the other people in the room, however, psychically "saw" her as an Indian woman giving birth to a child in breech position. The physical situation was so traumatic that both mother and child died. Barbara, who usually is in touch with her own inner pictures, saw nothing of this. She experienced only the emotions resulting from the healing energy passing through her. Soon after that session, Barbara had a reading with Gay. Gay told her that she had had many painful experiences involving children and childbirth. Relating all this to Sandy, Barbara concluded that "Perhaps I had to adopt first in order to have a child."

The second psychic experience happened during one of her meditations. She "saw" a light being carrying a shimmery blue sword. This being spoke messages to her about the upcoming earth changes. She felt at the time that the messages were to her and others simultaneously. She did get the personal message, however, that she was going to be "repositioned," that her family situation would soon change. It was a week later that she and her husband bought a new house outside of Philadelphia and just happened to contact an adoption agency. Adoption had not entered their minds until that point. They were directed then to the agency that provided the unusual service of allowing birthing mothers to choose the adopting families for their children. They met with the mother who had chosen them to parent her child twice before the birth. Barbara reports that she felt connected to this young woman, sometimes feeling like her mother, other times like her daughter. Then, fulfilling the prophecy that two entities would enter physical reality—perhaps not by totally "natural" means, and against all odds—Barbara herself conceived the second child around the birth time of the first. We certainly see here the mixing of psychic and physical realities to create the desires of determined beings.

Sheila had felt a feminine entity around her for many years. The birth of her daughter, Jaime Lynn, on December 13, 1985 is another story of an entity entering at the right time.

Sheila had been dealing with the issue of having a child as long as Sandy had known her. It had been a conflict between Sheila and her first husband because she had not trusted him, fearing that he would take the child away from her. The fear was strong even though Sheila had no outward justification for it at the time. Later when she and Sandy began their work with Gay, she learned of the unconscious influences that affected her.

Throughout many lifetimes, Sheila had had her children taken from her. Over the years, undergoing past-life regressions, she worked through many of these influences. This intense therapeutic work finally resulted in her marriage to a supportive, loving man and the birth of Jaime Lynn. The birth itself, however, dramatically brought to conscious awareness one of these lifetimes. Sheila was in intensive labor, her contractions about three minutes apart. Sandy and her husband, Alan, were coaching her through the labor, encouraging her to do her Lamaze breathing and rest between contractions. Suddenly she began to sob uncontrollably. Pictures of another time and place were flowing through her mind and she was unable to focus on the present. She could see herself in a primitive tribal setting, alone and in labor. Everyone was gone, probably dead. She had to deliver her baby alone and she feared that it would die. It did. The feelings of that memory were so intense, Sheila was unable to overcome them and focus on the present. She sobbed and sobbed.

A nurse burst into the room, asking, "What's going on here? Is she okay?" Sandy waved her away, assuring her that everything was under control. She had begun speaking in a hypnotic tone to calm Sheila so that she could assist her in dealing with these feelings. Sandy suggested that she go to her primitive self in that other time/space and comfort her, telling her that she, Sheila, was now doing what she could not do then and that that would help her. As Sheila began separating emotionally from the past-life self in order to comfort her, she then was able to attend to her present self. Soon she was back in control of her emotions and able to finish the labor of delivering her own child. When that moment came, Sandy realized that Sheila had created a wonderful event that over came all the many, many children she had lost in childbirth during other lifetimes.

Normally in the birthing woman experiences an urge to push. This urge comes from a complex set of hormonal and physiological circumstances which aid the mother in pushing out the baby. Sheila did not experience that urge. The medical staff told her that she would have to push the baby out herself. For the first hour or so, she pushed by herself with only Sandy's help pushing against her legs. There was little or no movement and Sheila began to tire. Different solutions were considered, including forceps, and drugs. She rejected them all. "I'll do it," she insisted. Sandy and Alan understood her determination. Nothing was going to interfere with the safe delivery of this child. She pushed and pushed. Help came in the form of a nurse, a midwife, and a female obstetrician.

During the last few minutes, as Jaime was making her entrance into the world, Sandy had a mental, above-the-body experience where she could look down on the entire situation. She was pushing on Sheila's right leg. Pushing against Sheila's left leg was a very earthy maternity nurse who had several children of her own. Pushing down on her stomach was a midwife who had delivered her own child during the past year. Gently pulling Jaime out was the obstetrician, the mother of several children. Alan stood off to the side. Sheila's nineteen-year-old stepdaughter took photographs of the event. Sheila had created everything she needed. The situation proved that she was strong enough to do this against incredible odds; she had a support system of strong, maternal women and a loving, supportive family. Later she told Sandy that now she knew she had the strength to do anything she wanted to do.

Jaime's birth was the culmination of years of learning for Sheila. During her therapy years, she had worked through the confusion and ambivalence about having children that had resulted from her own upbringing and her father's early death. Those influences, however, did not account for the extreme fear that surrounded her ambivalence whenever she considered the possibility. It was only when she began to become aware of the psychic influences affecting this decision that she truly understood that fear. During her first marriage, she had feared that her husband would take any child that they might have away from her. Looking back over the dynamics of that relationship, it is very possible that the fear was justified even though she had no "evidence" to support her fear. Later she learned that there were past-life experiences between them where he had indeed taken her child away. The issue was not settled with their divorce, however. Sheila continued to be ambivalent about motherhood and through the years encountered other past-life influences which reflected her beliefs about her ability to have and keep a child. The resolution came with Jaime's birth, which was influenced by Jaime's determination (Sheila had felt a feminine entity around her for several years) and Sheila's brave willingness to work through each layer of feeling and belief as it came to the surface.

Having children or not is something that seems so simple to many of us, yet it is often much more deeply influenced than we might have ever imagined.

Chapter IV

Children and Parents: Who Affects Whom?

About six weeks after Jaime's birth, Sandy became very concerned about Sheila. As a new mother, Sheila was nervous about holding her delicate and dainty seven-pound daughter. Sandy felt that was to be expected in the beginning. She remembered her own trepidation eighteen years earlier when her first son was born. She kept telling herself that Sheila would soon feel confident with the baby and take charge of the situation as she always had in other areas of her life. She easily took over a household with three teenagers coming and going after marrying Alan. Surely, Sandy reasoned, she would be her usual confident self again. Weeks went by, however, and the situation seemed to get worse, not better. The baby had colic from birth and cried constantly. Sheila's hands continued to shake whenever she picked up the baby. Sandy was unable to tell whether the colic caused Sheila's nervousness or the nervousness caused the colic. Neither of her sons had had continuous colic so she had no idea of how exhausted Sheila had become.

She also did not know at the time that, since Jaime's birth, Sheila had been feeling that her daughter did not love her, that she had had a child who could not feel joyful and who did not want to be with her. For Sheila, the situation was a nightmare and no amount of reassurance seemed to help. She desperately wanted to be a good mother and have a happy baby. She had begun to believe that it could not happen. She read every book available. All of her time and attention went to making motherhood work!

At the end of January, Sheila had promised Sandy that she would come to a seminar Sandy was giving for teenagers that she counseled in her private practice. Sheila was to talk to them about using their psychic and creative energies and then go into a trance to allow Gay to talk. It would be the first time that Gay had spoken since about a week before Jaime was born in December. Sheila was due to arrive at the office at eleven in the morning. At nine, she called Sandy and said she didn't think that she could come. As Sandy listened to Sheila explain that the baby had just fallen asleep and would be waking up at about eleven, needing to be nursed, she heard once again the fear and uncertainty in Sheila's voice. This was not the Sheila that Sandy knew. This Sheila seemed powerless to deal with a six-week old infant. Sandy suggested that Sheila wake the baby at ten-fifteen, nurse her, and be at the office at eleven. Sheila seemed surprised that she could do such a thing. That too bothered Sandy.

Sheila did come, however, and as soon as she entered the office, a change came over her. She was the powerful Sheila that Sandy recognized. She fielded questions from the room filled with curious teenagers, then allowed Gay to talk. Gay came through with a force of energy that let Sandy know that she wanted to begin working again, exerting her power, as well as Sheila's. As Sheila left, Sandy suggested that they have lunch the next day and that Sheila should bring the baby. She had decided that it was time to say something to Sheila. She had been quiet, deciding that it was none of her business and something that Sheila had to work out. However, she loved her friend too much not to offer some support. She felt that something was happening that had nothing to do with getting used to mothering.

During lunch the next day, the same pattern exerted itself. Sheila was nervous, her hands shaking when she picked up the baby. The baby fussed, then cried. Sheila became even more frustrated, trying hard to make the baby happy, finally crying herself. Sandy suggested that this pattern was not typical of Sheila and that she was certainly not being the powerful, confident Sheila who had spoken in their office the day before. She talked about what possible influences might be affecting both Sheila and Jaime. Sheila agreed to a hypnosis session with Sandy the next day.

Sandy sat across from Sheila and instructed her to go into a deep trance, signaling when she was ready for Sandy to begin. As Sheila deepened her own trance, Sandy found herself moving into an altered state of consciousness. She hadn't planned that, although she knew that often when she worked with clients, she would move into states of awareness that were broader and more open than her usual consciousness. This felt different, however. She began to feel herself and the chair in which she sat floating off the floor. She grabbed the sides of the chair and hung on as hard as she could. She didn't want to disturb Sheila's trance. She also knew that the effects that she was feeling had to do with the energy that Sheila was generating with her trance. So she held on. It got worse. She could feel herself vibrating and though her eyes were not open, she was also sure that she was at least a foot off the ground. This went on for what seemed like a very long time.

Then suddenly she was overwhelmed with tremendous feelings of sadness and loss. Sheila nodded. Sandy, as best she could through her tears, asked Sheila what was happening. Speaking in a calm, detached voice, Sheila began relating what she was seeing, scenes from another time and place where she was the mother of many children. She was very poor and constantly afraid that her children would starve. Jaime was born to her there, and to save her life, Sheila felt that she had to give her away. She did so but with tremendous grief. As she related this in a calm voice, Sandy continued to cry and to vibrate within great waves of energy. Through this, she directed Sheila to go to the woman she once was and comfort her, aiding her grief by showing her that she, as Sheila, in another time and place, was now with Jaime again in much different circumstances. After this was accomplished, Sandy then suggested that Sheila call on Jaime's higher self and communicate with her on that level, explaining to her that she had done the best that she could have in that other reality, and that she loved her very much and wanted to be with her now. Sheila did this, both she and Sandy crying by this time. The vibrating "levitation" feeling and the emotional intensity that Sandy was experiencing did not abate until Sheila was finished and came out of trance.

The two women realized that many levels of relationship were activated during the session. First of all, Sandy and Sheila's long, intense, and loving relationship had made it possible for Sandy to "take on" some of the emotional intensity of the situation so that Sheila could be free to do the work that was necessary to change the influence of a dramatic past life. Secondly, the complexity of Sheila and Jaime's relationship was evident. Each being was affecting the other. Jaime's anger and pain at being abandoned by Sheila intensified Sheila's guilt and subsequent feelings of helplessness while interacting with Jaime. Sheila reported that after the regression she was able to allow Jaime to be as she was, letting go of the tremendous need to make her be happy. She knew that Jaime needed to work through her feelings of rage, just as she had had to work through her feelings of guilt. Her nervousness left and people began commenting about how much more relaxed she was with the baby. Eventually Jaime's colic disappeared as she physically matured, and as she finished working through her feelings, further bouts of pain or discomfort were easily traced to some in-the-moment cause and effect, a DPT shot, for instance. As of this writing, at nine months, Jaime is a delightfully happy, laughing, crawling, clowning joy in Sheila's life.

In Sheila and Jaime's situation, each affected the other. Sometimes the situation seems to be balanced in one direction or the other. In the fall of 1984, Sheila did a session for a couple with three children, one severely crippled and mentally deficient. At the time of the session, this child was about three years old and had the mental and physical capacity of a six month-old-baby. This couple faced years of responsibility and care for a growing child who would always be an infant with no hope of improvement. They would not consider institutionalized care.

Gay focused most of her words on the interaction between the mother and child. As with Sheila and Jaime, there had been poverty in past lives and the mother, as the mother then, had given away her child. She suffered tremendous guilt. The daughter never forgave her, carrying much anger into this lifetime. On the psychological level, Gay explained, it would appear that the daughter's birth and the mother's determination now to take care of her was punishment for the earlier abandonment. On deeper, psychic levels, however, Gay went on to describe the daughter's "history."

She had many lifetimes in which she searched for love and then manipulated people to obtain what she thought was love, always left feeling that she was really abandoned. "She is," Gay announced, "quite aware at the levels of psychic interaction, that she, in effect, is controlling the entire family. She hopes that these parents will continue to sacrifice to care for her and thus she believes she is assured of their love. The learning here," Gay said, " has to do with learning to love from the heart, learning the true nature of love and that it is not necessarily in sacrificing." She went on to explain that the daughter needed to learn that, as a soul, she cannot manipulate others into loving her. The couple needed to focus on working with loving her from spiritual levels, and to let go on the physical plane, regardless of how that may seem to them on the surface, even if it eventually meant putting her in a nursing home.

Sheila had been interested to note the change in the mother during the session. She had come in angry and hostile, complaining that she was dragged there by her husband. She had started crying while Gay spoke, however, and later reported that she felt as if a "dam had burst."

It is difficult for most people to realize that even babies are responsible for their reality. On the surface, the infant in this family appeared as a helpless victim of the circumstances of a birth defect over which she had no control. And, on the surface, that is true. The emotions that each of us feels when confronted with such situations are a necessary and beautiful part of our personal learning. Our feelings enlarge us, expand our awareness, and teach us about who we are. And it is through these feelings that we can finally arrive closer to the God we all are as we learn to take responsibility for our own lives. The mother in the above situation "burst through the dam," weeping with relief, as she let go of her own guilt and accepted the deeper truth that her daughter, as she herself was doing, was creating a particular reality in order to learn and grow.

Each of us chooses the circumstances of our lives—the location, material surroundings, and relationships. In another session, Gay again went deeper than the obvious in order to illustrate how we do this, creating learning situations out of the stuff of our thoughts, experiences, and beliefs. A young man, whom we will call Larry, came to Mind Matters for sessions with Sheila and then with Sandy. He was an extremely sensitive person who had been having difficulty deciding the work he wanted to do in his life. He had been in and out of mental hospitals during his adolescent years. He explained that he believed that he had to be "disciplined," but then suddenly would go "crazy" and become "ungrounded." Gay described his relationship with his father:

"What happens here is an over identification with others. You feel perhaps too easily what others feel and this is because you simply are psychic. You have chosen to see this as a fault, as a defect, in your personality rather than seeing it for what it is: you are a very psychic individual. There has been difficulty in accepting this because of your relationship with your father. I feel that he, from the beginning of this relationship, was angry with you. You did not want to know this or see this and you tried very much to please this person. I am not certain that it is possible to receive approval here.

"Even your work was an attempt to find some approval; however, I see that he was in love with your mother in another lifetime and you became her lover and the jealousy continued into your present existence. I am not even certain that your father was aware of this anger, but I feel that it was difficult to please him. You might simply assume that he has very high standards and is critical, but I feel it goes much deeper than this. He has also definite concepts about what a man ought to be like and you never felt you quite measured up to this concept of, we will say, manly strength. You came into this existence to challenge these concepts, to allow yourself to accept yourself as sensitive and yet, you will find your strength as you accept your sensitivity. This is your challenge in this lifetime, to be both sensitive and strong."

Gay then went on to talk about past lifetimes that Larry had explored. In one, he had been born with club feet and no hands. He had permitted himself to be a psychic and offer guidance to the people in the small Norwegian village where he lived. In a different lifetime, he was born with a strong physical body and hid his sensitive nature from the world. It is this dichotomy that he chose to overcome in this lifetime and drew to himself a father who would push him into the learning that he needed. The simple explanation that his father was jealous of him because of a past love relationship would not satisfy the deeper need to understand his part in drawing to himself such a father now.

Another father/son relationship illustrates another aspect of psychic influence. A man we'll call Stratford came for a session with Gay in 1983.

He complained of depression and a sensitivity to "everything," including alcohol and cigarette smoke. Gay's explanation was fascinating:

"You are now tired of the depression and realizing that you do not have to be so unhappy; however, there is a general feeling of helplessness, of powerlessness against a kind of force that surrounds you as if you cannot fight back. Indeed part of that force is your father's energy, energy you have carried around for years. Your father has little understanding or tolerance for your way of living; however, he does feel jealous and what he has been jealous of is your freedom and your way of life. Even though he does not understand it, still he often wished he could do the things you did. For a long time he thought you were selfish, self-centered, and sent you this message. Over and over these thoughts were sent to you and began to penetrate, to sink in at the subconscious, that you indeed were selfish and, therefore, bad. Now I am not saying you are. Now I am saying your subconscious says this and you did not feel you deserve to fight back. To feel your power was not an option, and so you became depressed after receiving this message."

Gay then talked of some past life experiences involving his father that mirrored the drama they are currently enacting. In one, he had again been his father's son and had refused to carry out plans his father had made for him. This relationship ended with unresolved anger. Another time, his father was a business partner of his. He caught this business partner stealing from him and severed the relationship "rather quickly and with great animosity." Gay continues, "I feel, of course, you were drawn together to work these feelings out; however, they have stayed at the level of the subconscious, and you have taken upon yourself a role where you have felt guilt in relation to your father, felt you did not deserve what you have, your creative talents."

Gay then suggested that they go beyond this relationship with his father and "look at your soul's journeys." Here she explained that Stratford had had life-times before on the earth plane, but "relative to the time spent on the earth plane, the soul has traveled more in other realms, even in other galaxies, unnamed at this time. ... You, I feel, are not as accustomed as some souls are to the environment of the earth. I feel that there are new ways of viewing reality that you are learning. You are adjusting to the environment and certainly you might be more sensitive than many others. Indeed, you are quite sensitive and you have not totally accepted this yourself. When you begin to feel and know that it is all right to be so sensitive, then this will not even be an issue in your life."

Gay then referenced Stratford's sensitivity:

"There was a friend, perhaps a lover, a few years ago, maybe a little before the depression hit,who was also jealous, perhaps much in the same way as your father, and also sent similar thoughts to you. He was quite unsure of his own abilities and talents. Now I am saying this to make you conscious of how sensitive you are to the thoughts of others. Underneath, you have great desire to please others, and you want to do this even if it ultimately is a burden to you. You have this desire. Now this particular part of your nature, your personality, is not indelibly stamped upon you. However, you could step back and take another perspective. Often those who like to please do well in the performing arts. It is a place to channel this energy and so you would be going in a very good direction."

Stratford is an actor. He can change, Gay reminds him, and not be so sensitive to the thoughts of others and to his environment. He also can use this sensitivity to expand talents and abilities that he has not been developing to full potential. The relationship with his father, and particularly the effect his father's thoughts have had on him, have pushed him to a point where he needs to recognize his nature and grab his power back, by becoming the best expression he possibly can of who he is.

A woman came to ask, among other questions, about her health. She complained of extreme emotional upset manifesting in her physical body as a series of different maladies which kept her from being productive. She described colds, headaches, and so on. Her mother had died when she was ten years old. Her mother had had a hysterectomy at age thirty-three. The woman had had one the year before this, sometime during her thirties. She felt she was recovering and her business and creative endeavors were coming together for her, but her poor health remained a constant source of discomfort. Gay began with the following:

"We will begin this session with a discussion of your health. Obviously you are influenced by your mother and I feel you have carried a great deal of unnecessary guilt. Deep within, you blame yourself for her death and believe that you too must suffer. You do not want to be fully healthy for you believe that you cannot be happy as long as she suffers or suffered. Being healthy is being disrespectful to your mother, and here is where you are stuck! Consciously, of course, you desire health and energy. Subconsciously, you are still feeling guilty, that it is not right for you to be happy unless she is, and on the soul level where your mother's spirit resides, she is still unhappy and resentful of her own past suffering, and so you are not free.

"Concentrate on sending her love and freeing yourself from this relationship, then you will be free to proceed with a healing method. Any method that feels right to you works. You do not need to have me assign you a method, for the methods could even change as you change. What is important is to decide on a direction and put your total trust in that method. The healing through these methods work if you believe they do; and, for you, if you can see that your choice of suffering does not ease your mother's pain. It does not make any difference to your mother whether you suffer or not. She still makes her own choices."

Gay then went on to urge her to remember her feelings at the time her mother died. Often young children, still believing that the world revolves around them, believe that they caused major events in their lives. Gay even recommended a hypnotist for regression to that time in order for the woman to gain awareness of how her own thoughts created the belief in her guilt and the subsequent years of suffering. In this particular situation the mother did not seem to have an interest in affecting her daughter's health. The mother's state of consciousness, combined with the daughter's beliefs about her mother's death, brought on her continuing unhealthiness.

Influences between parents and children are often subtle and deep. They are always a reflection of learning that each has chosen. They are always open to healing whenever that learning is complete. Awareness of these influences hastens the learning and the healing.

Chapter V

Children and Parents:
Healing Together

Much of the psychic work Sandy and Sheila have done over the years, for themselves as well as for their clients, has involved healing in relationships. Sheila's intense psychic encounter with her newborn daughter, described in the previous chapter, is an example of such work. Reaching out to communicate at levels of being beyond the usual physical and verbal exchanges between people makes it possible for deep, far-reaching change to occur. In an altered state of consciousness, Sheila was able to "talk" to Jaime's greater being or "higher self." Over the years, Sandy and Sheila learned the value and effectiveness of such telepathic communication.

Raising children is a major learning process as any parent knows. Sandy's journals are filled with testimony to that learning. The stories often had a pattern. She would be working through some particular aspect of her personality (or concepts about what her personality was!) and, sure enough, there were her children, ready and willing to intensify the situation so that she was forced to face herself. At different times during the years of child-raising, the interaction between parent and children stood out even more prominently than usual. During the early adolescent years of each of her sons, Sandy found herself in accelerated learning situations.

Steven was about twelve years old when he first discovered that there were many flaws in his mother. Suddenly Sandy could no longer scramble eggs correctly. Everyone else in the world did it better than she did. Most of the time, Sandy took this change in stride, even laughing at the absurdity of his criticisms. Other times, however, it was not so easy. She had always thought of herself as an "insensitive" person. That "fact" was often reflected to her by those in her environment. (Of course!) During Steven's hormonal, adolescent period, events rushed at her that forced her to begin re-evaluating that self-judgment. These events culminated in a family crisis.

Griffin cut his foot on a piece of glass. Steven carried him home, rushing to the house, screaming in unison with his younger brother. Sandy stopped them at the door. The foot in question was covered with mud and blood and Sandy could not see the extent of the injury. She insisted that the foot be cleansed with the hose before the boys entered the house. Steven started yelling at her that she cared more about her damn rug than she did about Griffin's foot. Her reason told her that she was doing what needed to be done, and, that most of the time, these "emergencies" were not as serious as they seemed. Emotionally, however, she felt his accusation hit her right in the solar plexus. The cut was not serious and soon Griffin was back at play.

That night a serious accident did occur. She had just prepared a cup of hot tea and settled into a living room chair to drink it while reading the newspaper. Steven and Griffin ran into the living room excited about something that they had just discovered about Steven's new sneakers. He lifted his foot to show her and knocked the hot tea all over Griffin's left leg. Griffin was screaming with pain. So was Steven. A few drops had hit his socks and soaked through. He was not seriously hurt but Griffin was. Sandy picked up Griffin and rushed him into the bathtub to run the leg under cold water, then she applied aloe plant leaves to ease the burn. It was not as serious as it could have been and Griffin, who was eight at the time, soon relaxed and eventually fell asleep. Steven, however, continued to scream. Sandy knew he wasn't hurt but she sensed that he wanted her to think he was hurt to ease his guilt about spilling tea on his brother. She tried talking to him, but he simply screamed more, so she told him to go clean up the tea. Instead he chose to fall down the stairs. Again he wasn't hurt. In fact, one of his current games had been to fall down the stairs and laugh about it. This was another ploy for sympathy. Later, she did invite him to talk about his feelings and he proceeded to tell her everything that was wrong with her, most of it adding up to her "insensitivity." She was devastated and asked Gay about what was happening between her and Steven.

"The sensitivity is there but you do not believe this. Cut the psychic bond from your present self to your past self in this life. In many ways you still want to be treated as you believe you were as a child. Your self now can easily reach back, sending your child self love. Cut the tie that represents the so-called bad ways you were treated. Send love. Watch the past change. Focus on those who see your sensitivity and even your son's attitude will change."

It took Sandy weeks to complete this exercise. There was indeed a part of her that wanted to be "treated as you believe you were as a child," having always been told over and over that she was wrong, that she could not do anything right, and so on. She finally accomplished the separation from her own poor self-concept in this area, and indeed, she no longer heard that complaint from Steven.

Several months later, however, another pattern asserted itself, one that reflected even a deeper dynamic between the two of them. Sandy had divorced Steven's father when he was six years old. Over the years, he had displayed jealousy at different times toward her various male friends. This jealousy intensified, however, with the shifting hormones of adolescence. Sandy was seeing someone new in her life. The first time this particular man came to the house, Steven became moody and the next morning refused to go to school, claiming that he had a stomachache. This too had been a pattern of his and Sandy did not believe it was real. She sent him to school and he was fine. She decided, however, to ask Gay what was going on. She felt tremendous guilt over these various relationships and how they might be affecting her children. She asked about her guilt and Steven's jealousy.

"There is both jealousy and guilt happening simultaneously, each feeding the other. Your guilt is there, but as he grows older, the feeling is one of betraying your love for him. However, he also wants you to feel this way, thus assuring him that you do love him only. He wants to be the only one and this has been a source of much inner conflict. You see, it is simultaneous, for you each have beliefs and feelings that coincide. What you can do must be for you alone. This will end much of the conflict. It is necessary for you to believe that you do love Steven. Often you know you do love him but you are afraid he does not know. He knows your love but, because of other lifetimes, he constantly is trying to make you show him proof. This is not necessary. Concentrate even more on assuring him at psychic levels, particularly during dreaming and sleep states. Ask that your higher selves meet and resolve this conflict. You also must let go of attachments."

After talking to Gay, Sandy returned home to be greeted with another crisis. Steven's father rushed over to her, exclaiming, "Have you seen Steven? We had to rush him to the doctor. He cut his finger!"

Sandy felt paralyzed. She could see this incident as simply another in a long series of such happenings, all designed to make her respond the way Steven wanted her to. She told Bill to take care of it. An old thought about being insensitive and heartless took hold of her but she felt that she could not go to him and pretend to be upset. When he returned home, a butterfly bandage on his finger, she responded coolly. He complained and pouted. Later when she put him in bed, she leaned over to kiss and hug him, and with no mention of the finger, said, "I love you very much and you don't have to hurt yourself to know that." Before he protested, he grinned!

Sandy took Gay's advice and began working on this issue on psychic levels. A year or two later, Steven walked in on Sandy and a lover. Sandy was disconcerted and embarrassed but Steven brushed it off with, "Good for you, Mom." This incident showed her that the psychic work she had done was effective. At the time of Gay's words, however, she was not clear about "letting go of attachments." That she learned when Griffin reached his early adolescent crisis.

Griffin's thirteenth year was 1984. Early in the year, he began exhibiting an overall moodiness with unpredictable emotional swings. Sandy remembered Steven's adolescent struggles and settled in to take it as it came, knowing that it would eventually blow over. She did not know, however, that she had had it easy with Steven and now she was to learn how difficult the rites of passage from childhood to manhood could be.

Griffin stopped talking to her or anyone, except his two closest friends. With them, he took long walks in the woods where they whispered to one another with agonized looks on their faces. Disdainful responses met any inquiries from the adult world. Sandy felt closed out and disliked. Griffin had always been the child who talked about what was happening in his life. He always had given her the facts. In contrast, his brother had usually talked about his feelings but never about what was actually happening. Griffin had had difficulty talking about how he felt, but would chatter endlessly about what he did or what his friends did or did not do. This new quietness disturbed her but it was to get worse.

From the general moodiness, Griffin shifted to acting out with unacceptable behavior. In the course of several months, he got caught drinking beer (which he insisted he "found" in the woods, which, in fact, turned out to be true); smoking cigarettes (something Sandy had never done and certainly did not want for her young son); and finally, after the school year began, he got caught by the gym teacher with a small amount of marijuana. Sandy was devastated. She questioned her parenting skills. She worried about his future. She was sure that he would end up drugged out and alienated. Emotionally she was a wreck. She responded to him by yelling, pleading, crying, yelling some more, threatening, and crying some more. None of this worked. He would glare at her, refusing to say anything, to offer any explanation or even regret for his behavior.

Caught in the middle of her own crisis, Sandy forgot everything that she knew and would have advised her own clients to do. Fortunately, she had a network of friends who were there to put her back on track. One friend, Ginny Ramus, a trance-channel who speaks for an entity named Valoos, did a channeled session for her in which Valoos advised her to "cut the cords" with Griffin and give him some psychic space. Shortly after that session, Gay advised the following:

"I think you need to refocus yourself and to focus at an emotional, spiritual level and work from there; for at the physical plane, you are reaching the point where you cannot effectively control this. Now I know that this is frustrating; however, you may find that you need to let go of working at this from that physical level for I feel the time is coming when that may not be possible at all. Now you, of course, need to make clear to him what you want and expect on the physical plane, but then, to allow yourself some peace of mind, begin to concentrate on the spiritual plane.

"I feel that there is a battle occurring here between you both, and one that is not possible to win on the physical plane. So you need to let go of the battle, recognizing that you are fighting at another level, using different ways to accomplish this control. You, in a sense, are buying into his need to control his environment. He has felt powerless and this, of course, is influenced from other lifetimes. What he wants to do is control his environment, and you are part of that. To struggle with you is what he wants, and yet what he needs most is to let go of this. Now the problem is here, so you let go of this struggle. You realize this at times so you do let go and then he becomes frightened and more combative, and that's when you, as you would say, get sucked into the struggle again. Now at this moment of letting go, if you can continue to let go, you may find that the combativeness will die out. I think that you need to cut these psychic bonds and cords and establish a strong heart connection. Now I am not suggesting that you not guide him on the physical plane, but recognize that you get involved in his need to struggle with his environment, which comes from other lifetimes. He needs to know, to learn, that the environment is not something he needs to struggle with."

Sandy took two steps. First, she contacted a psychologist who specialized in working with adolescents. She arranged weekly appointments for Griffin that lasted about four months. Occasionally during those sessions, she would be invited in to participate. There she learned much about her complicated younger son. She learned about his struggle with growing up; his confusion about how to be a "man" since he no longer felt like a child; his anger at her feminine vulnerability because of the confusion this brought to him as he tried to define his own masculinity; his difficulty dealing with her expectations (which she found could be grounded in her own history and have nothing to do with who he was). She also learned how much he wanted structure and guidelines from her. During one session, he called her a "push-over," claiming that he could get anything he wanted from her. She was shocked at that indictment because she had always felt like a strong parent. She realized, however, that she was easy, that she made few clearly defined demands. She simply "expected" her sons to behave, to know how to behave. Her oldest son had always known so she thought Griffin should know as well.

About the time that Griffin was going through the therapy sessions, they also acquired a puppy. Griffin became the primary caretaker of this dog. Sandy watched as he disciplined the unruly animal. She saw him stick to the rules that he gave the dog in situations where she would have given in to the dog's pleading brown eyes and wagging tail. Along with the discipline, however, Griffin lavished affection and love on the animal, wrestling with him on the floor, hugging him, sleeping with him, talking to him with laughter and love. She knew that this was what her son was asking for. She responded to the lesson. She set out her rules, her expectations for behavior. She stuck to them and when they were broken, she reacted with punishment. She also lavished Griffin with hugs and kisses even when he would pull away. She knew that he needed her touch even though he may not have known it.

The second step she took involved working concretely and consistently on psychic levels. She began a series of exercises to cut the psychic "cords" or "bonds" that she had with Griffin, leaving some "psychic space" between the two of them. (These exercises are described in Chapter 15). She established a strong connection at the heart center, sending out thoughts and images of white light representing her love going out to him. With the practice of these psychic exercises, her extreme emotional responses quieted, and she reacted more appropriately in specific situations. The tears, the pleading, and the anger subsided. Griffin responded dramatically. In fact, she noticed his response almost immediately after she started the exercises. She would meditate, cutting the bonds, freeing him from her investment in how he should be in the world. He would come then into her presence with his mood and attitude completely changed. She was amazed at how well it worked.

Griffin is fifteen and a half at the time of this writing. He occasionally breaks a rule and still struggles somewhat with his environment, but his relationship with his mother is much smoother. He hugs her back and even initiates a hug or two now and then. His overall behavior has fallen in line with her values and expectations as he has chosen those values for himself. He seems to feel much less pressure from her and yet thrives within the structured framework that she has designed in response to his need. Sandy learned a great deal about balancing the responsibility of being a parent with the need to let go and allow her child to create his own lessons. The letting go is on the psychic and mental planes. When that is accomplished, the responses on the physical plane can become appropriate.

Sandy was a parent in physical life with a young child. She got stuck in wanting him to be a certain way and had to learn how to get out of her rut, thus helping him out of his. Sometimes that "stuckness" carries beyond the physical realms into after death states. A young man that we will call Harry came for a session with Gay. He was in the process of changing his career. For the past couple of years, he had been working in a business that his father than left him when he died. Before his father died, Harry had been involved in spiritual pursuits, much to his practical father's dismay. His father's death had called him back into the business world. He now wanted out. He wanted to pursue a career in the psychological/spiritual counseling fields. He was having difficulty finding his way out of the business and into the training that he desired.

Gay told him the following:

"Your father is definitely influencing what is happening now. He is fighting this kind of ending. He is attached on a mental-spiritual level to some of the things you are dealing with and I feel your father's spirit is stuck. Mentally, he argues with you. He always was rather stubborn. He thinks he knows what is best, but of course his mind is still back many years ago. I am not sure he approves of your life. Of course, that is his problem, but it influences you. You can help make this transition out of the business easier by speaking mentally to him. You can do this now and also before you sleep. Simply tell him that it is safe to let go and to move always toward the light. You have let go of many old feelings, and you can do this now easier than you could before. Send him love, and we (the spirits) will tell him to turn toward light, turn toward new experiences and love and let go. You might find you need to repeat this to him, and you might find this could ease the entire process. Things are stuck. It is important for you also to be clear about what is yours, at least in your mind, and to trust more in the universe providing for you. You will be provided for. There are great lessons in your own creativity and in your own talent to draw to you what you need. You must trust this."

A year or two later, Harry reported to Sandy that after this session, his perceptions shifted. He was in therapy at the time which, he said, also helped, but Gay's words changed his feelings about *having to be* in business, and within six to eight weeks, new possibilities opened. He found that, indeed, he was learning to use his own creativity in bringing about what he wanted in his life. By the time he and Sandy talked, Harry had established his own successful private counseling practice in a near-by town.

Harry's life shifted when he helped his father's spirit heal. Sometimes the healing comes from the opposite direction. In the spring months of 1982, Sandy's good friend, Margo, began thinking about her father who had died years earlier. Margo is a person who lives her life, as Gay once put it, "on the emotional plane, and you have asked to experience your emotions to the greatest degree possible, and so you do." Of all Sandy's friends, Margo delves the deepest into her inner self to learn about the workings of her reality. She has a need to know and understand her feelings and how they influence the patterns of her thoughts and beliefs and subsequent reality. She usually believes that she must do this by herself, often at great emotional cost.

During the middle of 1982, Margo found herself dealing with issues that surrounded her relationships with men. She was writing much in her journals about this issue and recording many dreams that seemed to be opening her to deal with this issue. One such dream involved a loving relationship with a man. She and the man were with a third person who remarked that they "seemed" to love each other very much. The man, with a matter-of-fact and accepting attitude, said, "Yes, but Margo always spirals off when faced with a real, loving situation." Margo was very pleased with this dream because she knew that he was right, but she felt that he still was willing to accept her in spite of her "peculiarity." She wrote in her journal, "Is this what I always wanted from my father?"

Sometime after this, she had a reading with Gay. She remarked that she had been thinking quite a lot about her father recently and wondered about it. She was quite surprised with Gay's words:

"You are indeed re-experiencing your relationship with your father. Your consciousness is traveling back in time. For you, this is something you have "chosen" to do in order to complete your relationship with him. When you travel back in time in your feelings and psyche, you enter into a state close to what the meditative or hypnotic state is and you stay there for periods of time. The trips are important now. Your father is on spirit planes where he has done much learning and is in touch with you telepathically. This began to happen within the last year. I feel that he wants to be closer to you before he focuses in another existence and so he has communicated a desire to bring peace to this relationship. Peace in your case does not come so easily until you have uncovered your feelings."

Later in the session, Margo asked, "My father is attempting to heal his relationship with me. Is there anything I can do?

"Be receptive to this idea. No relationship is finished until there is forgiveness and love. Of course other feelings are naturally there. You cannot deny them, but let them flow. Allow them their right to existence. Be aware though that he does desire clear love between you. Naturally that is influencing you now too."

Margo was amazed by this information. She had always felt it was her responsibility to do all this work, to fix everything about herself. That someone, her own father, wanted to help her with this intense internal work, surprised and pleased her. She had been given permission to feel her real feelings about him and about their interactions with her mother. She felt hope that she would be able to iron it all out.

Over the next few years, she opened more and more to the inner work. She went through a series of dreams about a baby. The first came soon after the session with Gay. She dreamt that she had a baby and took this baby to a doctor. The doctor was warm and compassionate and examined the baby. He told her that the baby was extraordinary but that it had jaw cancer and needed an operation. Margo accepted this news easily and with no emotional upheaval. Instead she simply felt the doctor's compassion and love for her and her baby.

Later as she thought about the dream, she realized that the baby was her and that she had done a lot of extraordinary work on herself but still needed to express openly more of her own feelings. These dreams about the baby continued over the years, and the baby continued to heal. Margo now reports that this intense period of her life, working cooperatively with her father on those levels, has led to healthier relationships with the men in her life, and a healthier acceptance of her own mixed feelings about both her father and her mother and how those feelings affect her present reality.

A dramatic tragedy brought to Sheila's awareness the need to do some healing with her father. One of her best friends lost a full-term baby. She started labor in the middle of the night quickly and with a rush of blood. Calling Sandy to help her husband drive her to the hospital, she also called Sheila to baby sit with her young daughter. When Sheila arrived, already upset about her friend's condition, she was thrown into further emotional turmoil by the sight of all the blood on the floor and rugs. After everyone left to rush to the hospital, Sheila undertook the task of cleaning up the blood before the child awakened in the morning. She was devastated by the blood. For days afterward, she found that she could think of nothing else. She also found that she had difficulty being with her friend even though she loved her and wanted to express her love and concern during this period of grief. She knew that her feelings had to do with her father's death so she asked Sandy to help her. She had always had a vague sense of guilt around the event of his death, feelings that told her that she "never did enough."

Sheila was sixteen when her father died of emphysema and lung cancer. He was forty-nine years old. He died suddenly, at home, and with a great deal of bleeding from his mouth. Sheila witnessed it all, feeling immobilized and shocked at what was happening. She had been close to her father and depended upon him for emotional support in her family.

Sandy led the entranced Sheila back through her life to the day of her father's death. She relived the entire scene, but from the perspective of her adult self. She watched it as if it were a movie. From this perspective, she was able to see her child self and the incongruity of her long-held inner expectations for herself in the situation and the reality of a shocked sixteen-year-old child. She would not have expected her own daughter to behave any differently. As the events unfolded, Sheila then began to see something that she had not been able to perceive before. As she watched her father being carried out on a stretcher, taking his last breaths, she saw him look at her with love. She realized that he, in death, had not expected anything from her and had simply loved her. It was she who had expected so much of herself all these years.

Sometimes it is our own self-judgment that keeps us from healing. Sometimes we can even blind ourselves to the most obvious of human potentials by our thoughts. Sandy underwent a healing experience with her mother that pushed her into a new perception of herself. Sandy has been alienated from her mother for much of her adult life. They would have polite conversations once or twice a year, exchange cards and gifts, but little more. Over the years, she had done much work in therapy and on psychic and spiritual levels which had given her insight and understanding into the dynamics of this relationship. She had come to realize that she had "chosen" this mother for purposes of learning and had even strongly felt that she could forgive her mother for the various events of her childhood which had caused her pain. She felt little or no love for her mother, however. She rationalized that she had learned to love other women and now had close, loving relationships with women instead of the older, competitive relationships of her youth. She felt that she had done as much as she could.

The deeper, guiding levels of ourselves, however, often push us to new levels of awareness. This is exactly what happened to Sandy. For years she had been in a difficult relationship with a man. She was always trying to get out of this relationship, or to make it work the way she wanted it to. A couple of years ago, she went to see a therapist about this difficult situation once again. The therapist very quickly led her back to her mother. She got annoyed. "I've done all the work there is to do on that relationship!" she exclaimed.

The therapist insisted. "You must forgive your mother."

"I've done that, over and over!" Sandy was angry.

"Then you must love your mother."

This time, Sandy was sure the therapist was crazy. "I can't love my mother. She's simply not lovable. How can I love someone who is so hurtful? I've learned to love other women. That's enough!"

The therapist told her to write a letter to her mother telling her everything that she's ever wanted to say. Sandy left the office thinking that she would never return to such a crazy therapist. A week later, she did return, to thank her for changing her life.

She went skiing in Vermont, alone. The second day it rained. She stayed in the cabin writing and reading. About eleven o'clock, she heard a voice in her head saying, "It's time to write your mother!"

She thought that was crazy but went to her writing materials and began anyway. She wrote. Halfway down the page she wrote that she had always wanted her mother to love her. That wasn't news. She knew that from all the therapy. She wrote some more. She began to cry. Finally she found herself writing that all she ever really, really wanted was to know that *she loved her mother*. When she realized what she had written, she began to cry harder. She sobbed for several hours. When she finished crying and looked around her, the world had changed. It was still raining but everything was bright and beautiful! She felt released from years of struggle. She realized that as long as she hid her love of her mother from herself, she had to believe that she, Sandy, was not lovable. Her mother did not have to be any certain way in order to be loved. In fact, her behavior and her personality, as judged by Sandy, were not lovable; however, here it was! Sandy loved her simply because she was her mother. That meant, of course, that Sandy did not have to do anything in order to be loved. She could let go of patterns that she had developed over the years of trying to make others prove that they loved her and of never believing that they did no matter how much they tried to prove it.

Later that day, the universe provided Sandy with a synchronicity that confirmed her learning. She was reading a novel. The protagonist was talking about his mother, describing her personality. He then said, "If she were not my mother, I would not like her; but because she is my mother, I love her."

Sandy's healing with her parent has been within herself. She still talks to her mother on the telephone several times a year and knows that they probably will not be close friends in this lifetime no matter how much she desires it. Her attitude and perceptions have shifted, however, and she feels much more positive toward her mother and allows herself feelings of love. She now knows that the love comes from within her and not from the outside.

Chapter VI

Psychic Bonds

We have physical ties to our families, blood ties that bind us to our parents, our children, and our cousins. Literature abounds with mythology about the "thickness" of blood, the loyalty within families, the importance of family honor, family name. We have seen that these blood ties are chosen at deep levels, people coming together as family to work through learning, to be together in love. What happens when we choose a lover? Are those choices any less significant because we cannot see the "blood" connection? Or do those connections also provide a deep learning ground for our human experiment? Again, we can look to literature for great stories of extraordinary relationships, such as Dr. Zhivago and his Lara; or we can pick up our daily newspapers for examples of such relationships.

In December of 1984, a mother and son "pleaded no contest to incest charges, conceding that they knew of their relationship when they wed and agreeing to seek counseling in return for staying out of jail." This man and woman met, fell in love, and married in spite of knowing that seventeen years earlier she had given him up for adoption. What kind of tie would pull them together in defiance of cultural convention and law?

SENSING HIS DEATH. . . (Associated Press)

PATTERSON, CALIF. A 15-year-old boy who learned that his girlfriend needed a heart transplant told his mother three weeks ago that he was going to die and that the young woman should have his heart.

Felipe Garza, Jr. who his half-brother said had seemed to be in perfect health, died Saturday after a blood vessel burst in his head.

His family followed his wishes, and Garza's heart was transplanted Sunday into Donna Ashlock.

His half-brother, John Sanchez, 20, said Garza told their mother three weeks ago: "I'm going to die, and I'm going to give my heart to my girlfriend."

Ashlock, 14, who also lived in this farming community 75 miles southeast of San Francisco, had just learned that she had an enlarged heart and needed a transplant. (*The Philadelphia Inquirer,* 1-7-86)

His wishes were granted and Donna Ashlock now lives, a testimony to Felipe Garza's love and uncanny sense of knowing his own impending death.

On a happier note, *The Philadelphia Inquirer* reported on December 11, 1986 that Alton Davis and Bessie Speicher, both 86 years old, were married in Seaford, Delaware. "The ceremony will cap a romance that began in 1916 but was thwarted by circumstance and, for many years, a distance of 3000 miles." It seems that Alton and Bessie had been high school sweethearts, "attending oyster roasts, picnics and private dances" through the years 1916 through 1921. Then in 1921 they broke up, "for reasons neither would explain." They each married and raised families, Bessie in Maryland, Alton in California. His wife died a couple of years ago and shortly afterward he learned of Bessie's whereabouts. He came courting and the wedding was on. Why after all these years? "I guess we kept that little spark burning all those years, and when we saw each other it started up again," Bessie reported.

What is that "little spark" that burns for forty years through the many changes that Alton and Bessie must have endured as they moved through their lives? Certainly they look different now, and certainly their personalities have altered, growing in some ways, becoming rigid in other ways as happens in the natural process of growing older in our physical world. And yet, that spark, that connection remains and they are happily back together. How do these "connections" or "bonds" work in the learning of our lives?

A young married woman came for a session with Gay to ask about her relationship with her husband. They were both teachers of meditation and spiritual concepts. They had separated for a short time while she went away to study. During the time she was gone, he became involved with another woman. Now they were trying to work through the implications of that event. They both wanted the relationship to work. Rather than address the affair, Gay talks about their karmic ties after describing how her psychological needs fit into the karmic learning:

"There are strong karmic connections of which I will speak later, but it is also important to understand your own nature from the psychological perspective. I feel that you are drawn to the struggle. You believe that you must earn affection and love through struggling. I feel the uncertainty here also provides you with excitement when you see him. I feel a strong pull together at the physical plane. I feel you are still in many ways searching for your father. I feel that this is still your desire.

"As I said the karmic bond is strong here. We will consider this to be other lifetimes. I see that you have been very close in other existences. I see this indeed was a very close relationship in the last century. I see you were lovers for many years. I think here though was much unhappiness, for you could not be open about this love. You were very wealthy and he came from poverty. Your father was of a very high rank in the military and you were not permitted to see your lover; however, many years you were together secretly. I see though that he finally left with someone else, and you then married someone your parents chose for you. I feel that despite this closeness you never really knew each other, for your meetings were beyond the daily existence. It was all romance and I am not certain either of you saw the other clearly. I also see you in Greece together. Here you studied philosophy and I feel that you admired each other but neither of you was able to approach the other due to feelings of great shyness. I see too that you lived in Russia where you were together in a small village in Northern Russia. Here you knew each other, for you were cousins, and I see you with him through a near-death crisis and saving his life. *I feel that you were drawn together in this existence to know each other, to have opportunities to be together and to learn about each other.* You are still not seeing each other in a clear way. You need to let go a bit and stop worrying about how you are "handling" this situation. You can not make a mistake here."

This woman came in because she was upset and anxious over her husband's affair and was afraid she would behave badly and lose him. Now she is told she cannot make a mistake. She hears that she needs to struggle in order to have love and affection. She also learns that there is a strong karmic tie with several shared past lives that have brought them to this moment. Earlier in the session, Gay also had talked about her husband's fear of closeness and lack of trust in women. This seemed to have more to do with his mother than with her, just as her need to struggle had to do with her father. Now Gay talks about how they "play out" these patterns together:

"Trust that he is not leaving. He is drawn to you also. I feel that he is not about to leave you but you may only know this after some time has passed. You are connected at a deep level. Many of the feelings you experience are because of what he is experiencing. Recognize too that you are often seeing yourself reflected in him, for you have also been twins before and you too have the same ambivalence and doubts. You do not have to think about this, for he expresses that part of the relationship. You express the part that seems to need closeness, so you both want to be close yet you both are ambivalent. You need to let go and to trust."

This kind of "see-saw" effect, whereby one lover expresses one need in a relationship and the other expresses the opposite or complementing need, is a common pattern in such deep relationships. These are people who know each other so well that they are unconsciously acting out behaviors and feelings for one another that go far beyond what normally might be expected. You will see many examples of how this works throughout this book.

A couple we will call Anthony and Jane came together for a session. Gay's words to them are an excellent example of the dynamics in a long-term, stable relationship. They were both concerned about their relationship and "where it was going."

"I feel that you are clearer in your minds than you wish to admit for you know what you want, but as soon as you become conscious of your individual desires, you decide that this might be in conflict with your relationship together and so many possibilities are ruled out before they are given expression. In your relationship together I feel that there is a balance of energies that you have both needed and asked for. ... You are both asking for the same thing although it may not appear so on the surface. What you both want is a feeling of freedom. What gives you this might be different and yet you need to understand that you are at a deep level asking for the same thing. You are quite different on the surface and yet you are mirrors for each other in many ways. What you see in each other is an unresolved portion of your own individual psyche, something that perhaps you have kept hidden. I feel that you have needed to have these differences in order to see who you are at a much deeper level. You may need to think about this for a while but I feel that each of you needs to decide what you want. If you want to be together, then it is quite simple. You need to let go of trying to help each other and simply love.

"You have been together before and I feel that there are several existences where you have been together and each of you has experienced leaving at a difficult time. You do though share a very deep bond and regardless of where you are this exists. This is what you must believe in. You both need to concentrate on what you feel is best for you as individuals, and while doing this, send love. Often people concentrate on what they feel is best for a "relationship" while sending anger and hate. You are learning here to do the opposite and you must trust in love's magic."

After Gay talked, Sheila and Sandy talked with Jane and Anthony at length about how people tend to not hear each other because they "think" that they know how the other will react and so hold back, anticipating responses that they themselves have predetermined. Each of these people had been trying to outguess the other, little realizing that they wanted the same thing and were "mirrors for each other." Anthony and Jane married a couple of years after this session. They are each doing their individual creative work.

Another example of a deep psychic bond between two people that "set up" certain expectations for behavior came through in a session for a woman we will call Marian. Marian met the man with whom she was living about the same time that she became interested in metaphysical and spiritual matters. Her lover was adamantly opposed to her new interest and constantly scorned and scoffed at her ideas. She felt a "mission" to change him and convince him that these new ideas were valid and important for his growth. First Gay talked to her about the changes occurring in her:

"You were raised to follow the rules and be a good girl. Although you had questions, still you strove to keep the questions hidden and do what pleased others. The questions, however, remained inside. The energy (the new psychic events in her life) simply acted as a catalyst to unlock the questions and awaken in you the desire to have more in your life.

"You and Hank have lived many lives together. You have been married many times. Most of these lives have been quite conventional, very quiet, and in fact, boring, but you endured for at deep levels you loved each other. You kept your questions hidden. I see you living quietly in Kansas together at the beginning of this century. Another existence in New England last century. You remained a housewife. He was a mailman. In another existence, he had a grocery store in Vermont. I see these times as rather uneventful but, as I said, you loved each other. When you met now this comfortableness and love was drawing you together. He simply never expected any kind of change in you. I feel this is coming as a surprise and it is quite difficult for him. I feel within you the sadness at this moving apart for you feel this apartness because you are developing psychically. It is important that you recognize that love continues despite what is on the surface and that you also cannot force him to change. Love continues despite physical separations and this you need to know. I do not feel in him now a desire to change. He may attempt to keep you as you were but that is already impossible."

Hank expected Marian to be a certain way. This expectation had developed over many lifetimes that were deep in his unconscious. He could not understand his extreme reaction to her changes. She, on the other hand, wanted desperately to please him as she had always done in their shared past. She could not turn back herself so she wanted to force him to change with her. They are once again married and the battle continues, although Marian has learned to let him be and continue her spiritual pursuits on her own, trusting the bond that Gay described.

Sandy experienced a similar situation. She has been in an on-again, off-again relationship with a man for years. When they met, they were both intellectual, academic people with similar views of the world. Sandy began changing in the mid-seventies and eventually left behind what she came to view as the restricted world of the intellect for the wider, more creative spiritual approach to life. Her connection with this man continues in spite of these deep philosophical differences. The differences themselves have led her to a deeper understanding of psychic bonds than would have occurred if the relationship had been easier. She has had to examine each event between them with a clear, critical eye in order to grasp its significance and potential learning, and yet at the same time not fall into believing his intellectual judgment that she was being foolish and gullible. Through the years of this relationship, Sandy was able to define the psychological and spiritual patterns that they enacted together; witness different psychic events that they would generate with their emotions; experience various regressions into past lives that often helped explain some feeling or behavior that she could not otherwise comprehend; and through it all, learn about the many levels of letting go that we humans set up for ourselves as we learn our true nature.

Psychic bonds between people are evident on physical and spiritual levels. Sometimes there is a discrepancy between the learning on one plane as opposed to another. Sandy worked with two different people who experienced great difficulty in a relationship on the physical plane but a depth of connection on spiritual levels that explained the willingness to struggle so on the physical plane. The first was a woman who does psychic healing work. Janet had been in a relationship with Bob for about six years. They had married at one point, but three days after the wedding he asked for a divorce. They found that they were unable to live together yet equally unable to live apart. Bob too is a psychic healer. When Janet and Bob worked together, they worked in harmony and with great effectiveness. They also enjoyed vacations together and had fun. Janet was extremely frustrated with this situation and came to see Sandy thinking that a regression might be of help. Interestingly, it was not so much the events of the past life that were helpful but the spiritual after-death realization.

Janet found herself in a "long dress" time period. She and Bob had been lovers. She had his child. He refused to marry her. In anger and desperation, she drowned their child. She cried and cried, saying that he had never forgiven her for this and that she could not forgive herself. Using her usual technique for seeking self-compassion and forgiveness, Sandy took Janet into an after-death state where she could view the event from a higher self perspective. There everything changed. Suddenly Janet could see that, on this level, Bob had forgiven her as she had forgiven herself. Somehow, however, that forgiveness has not yet been translated to the physical plane, and the dichotomy between what happens to them when they are in a spiritual state as opposed to the physical state was explained. Their healing work is done in a higher self, channeled state of consciousness. Living in the same house with its day-to-day physical routine, brought up old resentments and guilts.

The second situation involved a much newer relationship but a very intense one. Dorothy is a friend of Sandy's who lives in California. She is a prominent scientist who has accomplished much in her young life. She was visiting the Philadelphia area and asked Sandy for help with a new relationship in her life. She met Frank about two months prior to this session. The attraction had been immediate and intense. The "coincidences" of their meeting and subsequent courtship pointed to a deep connection. He had dreamt of her before their meeting. He found it easy to pour out his feelings and his history to her, whereas he had always been extremely private and to himself. He wanted her to move in with him. She was reluctant but with his urging finally did so. She wasn't there a week before things started going wrong. He pulled away emotionally, distancing himself from her. She didn't understand what was happening. He asked her to move. She was floored but did so. Now he wanted her back.

Sandy suggested a hypnosis session to get in touch with their connectedness in order to understand the dynamic. She put Dorothy in a trance and set up the procedure which would help her gain information about their connection and, gain some psychic distance by cutting those psychic connections. When Sandy reached the heart connection, Dorothy began to expand her consciousness. By the time they reached the crown or spiritual connection, Dorothy was up and out into the reaches of her higher self. There she experienced herself with Frank. They were together, working on spiritual planes in peace and harmony. "We are bigger than life," she said, "I don't know how to explain it any other way."

She looked down from that perspective to the earth plane. There she could see her physical incarnation frustrated with trying to contain the reality of this connection in the limitations of physical reality. She witnessed Frank's frustration as well and saw that it was greater than hers because he did not seem to have this awareness that she was now experiencing. She realized that they were connected in what we might call "higher planes" of reality but had not yet learned to relate in a material, physical way. They were both overwhelmed by the connection and hence the ambivalent and yet intense feelings and behaviors. Evidently, they had not had many incarnations on the earth plane together and had not learned how to be together in that way. She went back to California with a sense of the work that they needed to do now.

Whether two people are learning to live together or be apart, the learning always involves some kind of letting go of old concepts, perceptions, prejudices, fears, guilts, angers. Months after the session quoted above, Gay said to Marion, "In every relationship, letting go always exists and yet on another plane, you always remain together; however, from the level of the person, as opposed to the soul, there is always letting go. No relationship stays forever at the person level. Of course, two souls can be together always." This concept was dramatically illustrated by Jo and Elaine's relationship.

Both women had seen Sandy for counseling. They had lived together for five years but that relationship had ended. Elaine seemed to have a harder time letting go than Jo did. Elaine would often push for more time together, for signs that Jo still cared, even for another permanent commitment. Jo was always feeling that she should take care of Elaine in some way or another. She would say that they needed "to talk." Elaine would then think there was hope for the relationship, only to be disappointed when nothing came of it. They worked through much of this in therapy separately. Jo went on to another relationship, but Elaine continued without a viable partner. Toward the end of Elaine's therapy, they decided that they would undergo a joint regression. They were feeling clear with one another and insisted that, at this point, there were no major issues but that they did feel a "constancy" in their relating that was important and they thought it might be helpful to explore it.

A joint regression is possible between two people who are connected at deep levels, having shared past lives together. Jo and Elaine had heard from various psychics and experienced in individual regressions, information about their various shared past existences. Now, under hypnosis, they wanted to experience one of these lives together.

Sandy relaxed them as they lay side by side. After suggesting that they visualize light at various energy points along their physical bodies, she asked them to think about a time in their relating when they each felt especially close to the other. She urged them to concentrate on that feeling of closeness, then suggested that that feeling be a cloud to carry them through time and space into the shared past lifetime which was most important for them to review at this time.

Jo started talking first. She could see a plain with tall grasses. She was an African warrior out on a hunt. A tall, handsome black man, she/he carried a spear. There were several tribes hunting on this plain. Off to the side, out of sight, tied up and lying in a depression or pit was a captive male child. Jo could sense his presence and she intuitively knew that the child was Elaine even though she/he could not see into the pit. A large cat was stalking the pit, moving in for the kill. Jo knew that she had to save that child even though the child was not of her tribe, not even a captive of her tribe. She ran, spear in the air, screaming as she charged the lion. The lion turned and attacked her, wounding her before she killed it. She passed out and was carried back to her village to heal there. She never saw the boy in the pit. She lived a long life as did Elaine, then the boy. They were not to meet again in that lifetime.

Sandy took them each through death and into the spiritual space that opens up immediately after death. Here they were able to review this major event in a past lifetime and understand its significance on the soul level. Both women were crying. They realized that the nature of their bond was so deep that they did not have to "see" each other in order to feel it and act upon it. It no longer mattered that they were not together now as lovers. A greater letting go occurred as they knew, on all the levels of their being, that despite their physical separation, they would always be psychically bonded. A year or two later, Elaine committed herself to a new relationship with another woman. Jo and Elaine now see each other socially whenever the occasion arises. They have each let go of the old patterns between them.

Some writers have referred to the lovers experiencing these psychic bonds as "soul-mates." Sandy and Sheila preferred to approach such connections in a less restricting manner. It is possible to have several relationships in a lifetime that have the depth necessary for the intense learning described above. Awareness of these bonds and a willingness to explore their manifestations opens us to the rich and intricate tapestry of our total experience on the physical and spiritual planes.

Chapter VII

"Haven't We Met Before?"

When Ros met Dan, her heart stopped! Here was the man she had been waiting for. She felt a strong sense of connection to him. He was handsome, successful, charming, and available. They began dating and everything was perfect. Ros began making plans, day-dreaming about their wonderful future together. Not quite consciously, however, she also started guarding her words, planning her behavior, holding back her natural responses, all in an attempt to please this new man, to insure that he would want her. She constantly thought about what he might be thinking, what he might want, what would please him. She tried to do everything "right!"

Weeks passed and Ros was sure the relationship was cemented. He was so attentive to her, so caring. True, he had not made a commitment or even indicated that she was his only lover, but she was sure of herself. After all, she was doing everything exactly as she thought that he wanted her to do it. Then the other woman appeared. In a short, rushed telephone conversation, he explained that his old girlfriend, Paula, was back in town and he felt that he had to see her on the weekend. Ros was crushed. She couldn't understand what had happened. She came to talk to Gay:

"You and Dan have been married in another life and Paula was there also. He left you after many years of marriage to be with her and he wanted you to believe it was your fault. You were a sloppy housekeeper. You clung to guilt and you believed that you deserved what happened, so much so that you did not even ask him to support the children. You lived with guilt about this particular man and I feel that your desire in that life was always to recapture the joy of courtship and you fantasized him loving you in this way again. You did not marry again or even come close. Now in meeting him in your present life, I feel this tension arising in you. There is a fear of not pleasing him, but we must now look with some compassion here and recognize that this aspect (past-life self) of yourself, in a sense, was allowed to take over."

Ros, a beautiful, self-confident woman, impresses those who know her with her spontaneity and charm. She is successful in her work and in her personal friendships. The response to Dan was out of character for her and surprised her friends. She was suddenly unsure of herself, trying too hard to please, and was much too quick to blame herself for what was happening. Gay urged her to concentrate more on what she wanted in this relationship and to "let go of judging whether you have been right or wrong in your approach."

When a past-life self bleeds into the present, sometimes the only way to alleviate the influence is to become aware of it. Ros may have eventually come to realize the incongruity of her behavior around Dan without the past life awareness, but it was certainly easier once she knew the influence. Lori's response to a similar experience took more time.

A tall, beautiful woman married eight or nine years to a doctor, Lori came to see Sandy because she wanted to leave her husband. She had wanted to leave him for the past three years. "Help me do it," she pleaded. Sandy questioned her closely to be sure that she really wanted the separation. She did. When asked what was stopping her from doing it, her only answer was "roaches." She had had roaches in her apartment before marrying him and was afraid that she would find herself back in the same economic condition. Her husband was ten years older than she and quite successful. She attributed her reluctance to leave him to the financial security that he offered. She also expressed a strong fear of loneliness. She was afraid of being alone and having no one in her life. As she and Sandy discussed what she wanted for herself, concentrating on Sandy's favorite question, "What do you want?" she continued to lapse back into what she did not want—roaches and loneliness.

After a while, Sandy began to feel that there was something unspoken or unavailable to Lori's conscious awareness, and she suspected that it had to do with Lori's husband and his needs. Lori's presence and behavior in the world certainly pointed away from loneliness and poverty. She was beautiful, had had several extra-marital relationships, had a college degree, and worked in a responsible administrative position. When Sandy voiced her suspicions, Lori became very defensive and insisted that she wanted to leave her husband and wasn't concerned with his needs but only with her own. Sandy talked about subtle influences such as telepathy and past lives that they might have shared. Lori did not think this was possible.

Sandy decided to do a psychic cutting between Lori and her husband. She did not explain what might happen but suggested that the exercise might help "clear the air." Lori agreed to do it and settled down into trance as Sandy spoke quiet words of relaxation. Lori easily visualized the connections of light between her and Robert. Everything was predictable until she reached the throat connection. The throat center is the energy point concerned with self-expression and communication. Here Lori experienced "lumps" that refused to go away. She got the message that these "lumps" were protective in some way. When Sandy had her cut the light cords and visualize Robert moving away from her, the "lumps" simply dissolved. Sandy felt that her suspicions were confirmed, and that Robert was influencing Lori in subtle ways in order to keep her with him. She suggested to Lori that her fear of loneliness was his and not hers. She was quite surprised by the suggestion and said that she would think about it.

During the next session, Lori talked about finding an apartment which had everything she wanted. Instead of being pleased and excited, she was upset and agitated. Sandy suggested another exercise in which Lori would go back through her past to important choice points and fantasize about taking the other choice instead of the one she had actualized in her present life. When Sandy told her to fantasize not marrying Robert, she immediately blurted out, "But poor Robert! He'd be so crushed."

Sandy quickly responded, "Okay, we've got it. That's what's stopping you from leaving him. Let's do a regression." Lori was so startled that she complied and almost immediately moved into a trance state.

She easily moved into a past life situation in a Western setting where she was a female wearing a long calico dress. She felt out of place with her family and very alone and lonely in life. As she progressed through the lifetime, very little happened to change these feelings. She never married and eventually lived alone. Then she met an old woman who treated her kindly and became her friend. This woman became the most important person in this lifetime, and much later, when Lori's past-life self died, the old woman was the person there to greet her.

Since Sandy had given Lori suggestions to find a lifetime that she had once shared with Robert, she kept Lori in the after-death state of consciousness for a lengthy time, constantly asking her for the significance of the lifetime and its effect on her present life. Finally Lori realized that the old woman was Robert and that she, Lori, was now looking for that old friend in who she/he is now. She also realized that she deeply felt that she owed him for his/her kindness then. In her present life, the situation was reversed. Robert was the one who felt alienated and alone. He had few friends and clung to her for what comfort that he allowed himself.

Sandy did some letting go exercises but she wasn't sure that they were working in Lori's situation. She realized that the most important result from the session would be Lori's eventual realization of Robert's influence and her ability to express herself positively. Lori needed to realize this before she could take the steps necessary to free herself from a relationship that had not worked for several years.

Lori had one more session with Sandy in which she went into trance and had a dialogue between her head, the intellectual part of her, and her heart, the emotional part. Both parts agreed that she needed more time to digest this new information. Lori is a cautious, conservative person who makes changes slowly. Sandy urged her to honor those characteristics and suggested that she would now take the steps that she desired in her own time.

A year later, Lori made an appointment to see Sandy in order to delve into some work-related issues. Sandy was surprised and pleased to learn that Lori was now living on her own and developing new relationships. Lori reported that she had soon begun to see how Robert influenced her telepathically. She related an incident where she had felt an overwhelming urge to contact him late at night. She thought that it was her neediness and fear of loneliness. She could not reach him until the next day. It turned out that his mother had died that night and he needed her! "I'm seeing what you meant last year," she said.

Over the years, Sandy has explored a number of different lifetimes that have impinged on her present and particularly on her long-term relationship with a man we will call Len. At different times during these years, different lifetimes would appear, explaining a particular situation or feeling state that Sandy would currently be "working through." Because of its complex nature, this relationship has given her an opportunity to learn about the deeper and subtler influences that affect all of us. In the early years of her work with Sheila, Sandy was dealing with a strong feeling that she had concerning Len. Like Lori, she too felt as if she owed him something. At the time, he was withholding his presence and feelings from her, and she could not understand why she felt she owed him anything since his behavior was so hurtful to her. In fact, if anyone owed anybody in this relationship, logically it would have been the other way around. Sheila suggested that they do a past-life regression. Sandy agreed, and during her meditation she began to receive images of a rocky hillside with ancient open buildings. That evening as Sheila quietly gave her suggestions of relaxation, the images grew bolder and brighter. Soon she found herself in an ancient lifetime somewhere near the Mediterranean Sea. She was a woman of power, some kind of priestess or seer. She had been raised from birth to fulfill her position which seemed to be handed down from generation to generation within a particular family.

As Sheila asked her questions about her experience, Sandy began resisting answering. The pictures unfolded deep within her mind and she became more and more agitated. She could see Len there, a beautiful young man whom she loved very much. He was a poor man, however, and her position forbade a marriage. They had a child. He begged her to give up her power and run away with him. She refused. She liked the power she had. He ran off with the child. She was furious and sent soldiers after him to kill him. After his death, she raged with remorse and grief, ultimately killing herself in a pool of water with a knife. The blood ran red in the water, and that was the image that stayed in her mind as Sheila counted her up out of the trance. "You were certainly reluctant to give me any information," Sheila remarked.

"I feel so ashamed," Sandy replied. "I didn't know that I had that kind of murderous rage in me. No wonder I feel as if I owe him."

Over the years, Sandy witnessed other lifetimes where the violence between her and Len was reversed. She could see a balancing taking place in their relationship, reflected in the past-lives as they came up. Years later, she did a regression for "the fun of it" because she was going to teach a course on reincarnation and wanted to have a recent experience to keep her in touch with her students' responses. She was shocked when she got in touch with a pattern in her relationship to Len that had been unconscious.

Sheila took her back through time and space, seeking the lifetime that her unconscious deemed most relevant at this particular point in her life. This is a standard form for most regressions, unless there is a particular goal or a problem needing a solution. Sandy soon began to see herself living as a young woman in a small pioneer Western town. She was married to the town's storekeeper. Her life was pleasant but boring. Then she met a man, a rugged loner who was simply passing through town and stopped in her husband's store. She immediately fell in love. All of her thoughts were centered on this man. He would come into town a couple of times a year. Eventually they had an affair which continued for many years. From the moment that this man entered her life, the pioneer woman focused totally on the infrequent moments she would spend with him. All other aspects of her life faded into the background—her husband, her children, the community. As Sandy remembered the events of this life, the only important happenings centered around this man. His name was George. He died before she did, and the remainder of her years were spent in silent grieving. She could share her grief with no one and no one knew her complete obsession with him.

Sheila took Sandy through death into the after-death state to review the lifetime. As soon as she crossed over, Sandy recognized George. He was waiting for her. She was shocked to realize that George had been Len. That possibility had not occurred to her throughout the entire regression, even though George was Len's middle name in this lifetime! After she returned to normal, waking consciousness, she shook her head and said to Sheila, "I didn't even realize who George was. I was so obsessed with him and so much in the moment of the regression, I could make no connections. It makes sense, though. I've pretty much done the same thing in this lifetime. Ever since meeting Len, I have measured time by the events that have involved him. I do know, however, that I have been changing that. I guess I needed to see this other lifetime in order to realize how that relationship has obsessed me. I had no conscious idea!"

Vicki and John's experience exemplifies how past-life therapy can be useful in dealing with present life situations. In their case, it was marital struggles. Vicki and John had been married for about six years and had two small children. John is an extremely successful doctor in the Bucks County area. Vicki is his beautiful helpmate, in the office as well as at home. By most standards, their marriage was fulfilling and happy. These two people, however, seek the very best in everything that they do. They came to see Sandy in order to look into past-life influences. There were certain subtle feelings between them that sometimes marred their present relationship, feelings that could not be explained by their present lives. Vicki sometimes felt that John contributed everything to their success, that she had little real power in the face of his tremendous energy. This resulted in a holding back on her part which she recognized as resentment of his abilities and energy. "I find it difficult to communicate my feelings to him," she explained. "He's so overpowering and seems to always know what to do. I feel lost in it all."

John talked about his need for her and his fear that he would lose her. He most appreciated her physical beauty and her intelligence and couldn't understand why she felt as she did. Sandy suggested that they do a joint regression, going into the past together to discover their connections and any influences that may be affecting them now.

Sandy connected them together at their energy points and then suggested that they ride a cloud of "good memories" back into the past, where their unconscious would take them to the most important lifetime. Vicki found herself in a place that she was sure was Atlantis. She was in a group of people of which John was one but she was not especially with him. This group of people seemed to have an important message to convey to others and were engaged in activities to bring this about.

John found himself in a completely different place. He was on a boat writing a letter to Vicki whom he was leaving, swearing to return. Vicki immediately switched and tuned into where he was. She said that she knew that he would never return. He did not. She had his child, unbeknownst to him, and lived alone, never marrying. She was an outcast from her 18th Century upper-class English family. The family supported her economically but not emotionally. Her son did support her, however, and was with her when she died peacefully of old age. John, in the meantime, went to France where he became a doctor, married, and had several children. He enjoyed his life and seemingly forgot about Vicki. When it came time for him to die, however, he died in great distress and pain, fighting death with all his strength. When he finally passed over, Vicki was there and the reunion between them was emotional and joyful. They talked and John explained his fear of returning to her because of her family. She now felt as though she understood.

Sandy then directed them back toward the Atlantean life. It was at the time of the great destruction of this continent. Vicki saw the destruction coming and chose to die, easing out, once again, peacefully and by choice. John stayed and tried to impart the groups' message for the population. He was unable to do so because he was trapped in a collapsing building and crushed to death. Once again, he struggled with death, feeling it physically during the regression as a sharp pain in his stomach. Sandy urged Vicki to go to him and help him pass over into spiritual realms. She did and with the help of her presence and her soothing words, he finally let go and moved into spirit, the pain immediately leaving his stomach.

When they came out of the trance state, John remarked, "I've lived with that pain in my stomach all my life. It makes so much sense." They talked about the ramifications of the experience. Vicki realized that although John does the care-taking on the physical plane, she has always done the care-taking on the spiritual plane. He could see that he needed her special kind of ease in letting go and accepting. He is always so intense in everything that he does in his life, it does seem as though he has a message that he must impart. In this life, that message is about health issues. He often makes public speeches and presentations on preventive health measures. He believes that what he has to say is of extreme value and feels a compulsion to express himself. That is wonderful for his public and his patients; however, holding on so tightly has brought him physical distress. Vicki also realized that part of her holding back and lack of trust was the fear that he may leave her and not come back.

A year later that situation was reversed. Vicki and John came to see Sandy because he was fearing that he may lose her and wanted to know why. When they arrived, he reported that he had not felt the abdominal pain since their previous session. Vicki reported that she was feeling much better about her role in their marriage and was doing more of her own creative work. This time they wanted to experience a positive lifetime together. John expressed his fear of losing her and she casually remarked that she had an overwhelming fear of the ocean and wondered why.

Once again Sandy relaxed them, connected them at the energy points and moved them back into a past life. Vicki found herself on a boat that was pulling into a port. She was female, but disguised and hiding so that she would not be seen. She was gathering together some papers that were extremely important to her. As Vicki watched her previous self doing these things, she realized what it was about. She had left England to go to France with her lover. Her father had spurned her and disowned her. He was now dying and she wanted to see him once again. John was on the dock and saw Vicki, helping her off the boat. They did not see each other for many years after that. Vicki returned to her dying father and reconciled with him. He left her a fortune. She remained in England, a rich and successful woman who lived comfortably and happily.

John, in the meanwhile, was also a successful businessman. Years after their first encounter, they accidently met on the street. There was a deep, but unconscious, recognition. They courted and married. This was a late-in-life marriage with no children but extremely comfortable circumstances. They were joyful together. After a few years of marriage, he had to take an ocean voyage for business reasons. He urged her to come along because he was so afraid that he might die at sea and never see her again. She agreed and went. He, however, did not die. She did, drowning, trapped in her heavy Victorian clothing which pulled her down into the water. Her experience before dying was traumatic but once again as soon as she crossed into spirit, she felt at peace. John survived and died a few years later of a broken heart. She met him after death. This time, Sandy suggested that they go to the past-life selves in their present form and have a conference, pulling together everything they needed to learn from their experiences. They talked together as Vicki and John and as their previous selves, discussing trust, fear, and how they are doing it differently now.

Recognition of these deep influences, whether one believes that they literally happened somewhere in time and space, or whether one believes that they are metaphorical and symbolize the circumstances of the present, brings an understanding and acceptance to the subtle interactions between people who are connected by bonds with a depth that we are only now beginning to comprehend.

Chapter VIII

"Who Me? Thinking of You?"

Sandy's friend, Len, was away. She had talked to him earlier in the week and he had told her that he had to go to Atlanta on business. He would leave on Thursday and return sometime over the weekend after stopping to visit relatives in Virginia on the way home. Consciously she did not expect to hear from him, yet all day Saturday she had a "feeling" that he would be calling. She kept dismissing it as "fantasy" or "wishful thinking" but the feeling persisted. Finally, about four in the afternoon, he did call, suggesting that they go to a movie. "I knew you were going to call," she said, "but aren't you in Georgia?"

He couldn't resist throwing one of her favorite complaints about him back at her, "You never listen to me. I go to Atlanta next week, not this week."

Sandy laughed and once again realized that she needed to trust that "feeling" when it comes over her because it is usually right, even when it's not! Sometimes he doesn't call even when she feels that he will; however, she has learned that when he doesn't act on his thought or his intentions, she nonetheless has accurately sensed what they are. This "communication" between them is sometimes funny, sometimes infuriating, and occasionally dramatic.

During a particularly busy time a few years ago, Sandy had not seen Len for several weeks. They had talked on the phone but had been unable to be together. Again, one Saturday, she kept "expecting" him all day long even though she knew that he was attending an all-day conference on the other side of Philadelphia, after which he was to go to a family party. The feeling persisted in spite of her reason. She went to bed at about eleven. As she drifted off to sleep, she began feeling a presence in the room with her. Her bedroom door was closed and the light was off. She lay on her side, facing away from the door. As she felt the presence, she tried to fight her way up from the level of sleep which she had reached. Although completely conscious, she was unable to come "up" physically. Her heavy body would not move. She then felt the "presence" embrace her from behind in a long body hug. She began to panic and yet she was also thinking that Len had arrived. She wanted to speak but could not. Her body would not function in a physical way. Then she "heard" his voice in her ear, "It's okay. It's just me. I'm here." She relaxed and turned over on her back, feeling his presence laying on top of her. She struggled to open her eyes. No one was there but the room was filled with purple light. The light lasted for what felt like a very long time, though it was probably no more than a minute. When she was completely out of the trance-like state she had been in, the room was dark as usual and empty. She felt wonderful, however, and "knew" that Len had been there. She fell into a deep, comfortable sleep.

The next day, in her journals, she speculated about what had happened. "My imagination? wishful thinking? a psychological need expressing itself? Maybe all those things were operating but perhaps more as well. My need is evident here, I wanted to be with him but that's always true. I think the emotional intensity between us the past few days brought about this event. I suspect that he wanted to be with me no matter what he was doing, but, as usual, wouldn't give in to the impulse. He seldom trusts his spontaneous urges. Perhaps his desire, matching mine, created a psychic event that I could consciously perceive because I'm open to such experiences. I'm sure such events occur more frequently than we perceive because of our cultural bias. I'll be interested to see if he was thinking about me."

A week later, they went out to dinner. She asked him about the previous Saturday night. "Did you think about coming by?"

"Yes. I did think about it but my daughter showed up at the dinner so I stayed much later than I had expected to. In fact, I had planned simply to come over and surprise you after the family get-together. I was disappointed but we had started talking and suddenly it was two in the morning."

Sandy told him what happened to her and he laughingly remarked that she would have to write the incident into her next book. Len is very skeptical about such events even though they occur regularly within the relationship. During that same dinner, a few minutes later, he asked if she could guess who had called him that week. Sandy spontaneously blurted out the name of a woman whom they both knew and with whom he had been involved years before. He had not heard from her in several years. His jaw dropped. "I must have told you before."

"No, you didn't. I just knew."

"That's uncanny," he replied. Then he started testing her by asking where some woman that he had met recently was living now. Of course, Sandy had no idea and when she thought about it later, she realized that the telepathic "knowing" that occurs between them usually involves some kind of emotionally charged issue. In past years, she had been jealous of the woman who had called and still did not like hearing that she would call occasionally. She wasn't interested or concerned about where some stranger was living.

An "emotional charge" was certainly a factor in two incidents that occurred with one of Sandy's clients, whom we will call Jody. Jody is an attractive, highly sexual woman with consistent and accurate psychic ability. She has learned over the years to trust her psychic "messages." The incidents that she reported to Sandy were highly emotionally charged, yet each was very different. The first event involved a delightful experience with a lover. Jody had been staying with her mother for a couple of weeks, helping her get ready to move to a new apartment. She had been away from Ed during that time and missed him very much. Her mother suggested that she look through some discarded clothing and take what she wanted. She found a beautiful see-through peach negligee that was dated but had potential. She shortened it, restyled the sleeves and loved the results.

About eleven-thirty that night, she was alone in the guest room of her mother's house. She kept thinking about Ed. Looking up, she noticed the negligee hanging on the closet door and began fantasizing about wearing it for him. She could see the flimsy material shimmering in the soft light from the hallway. She laid back on the bed and imagined a clear picture of the living room and hall that led to the bedroom where Ed would be at that hour. She then saw herself there, dressed in the peach negligee. She felt it flowing lightly against her skin as she moved down the hall toward the bedroom. She could feel the excitement and anticipation of seeing him and of him seeing her in the negligee. In her fantasy, she walked through the bedroom doorway and over to the foot of the bed where Ed was lying. She smiled at him. As he followed her with his eyes, she could see the warmth and appreciation in them. A loud noise jerked her back into the awareness of her mother's house.

Fifteen minutes later, Ed called her. He excitedly told her that he was lying in bed and "saw" her in his bedroom wearing a flimsy coral nightgown. He said that it seemed so real that he had thought that she had come to surprise him. He described how she had stood in front of him, then suddenly "flowed" out of the room. He had gotten up and searched the apartment, convinced that she was there.

Jody had been "sending" Ed strong, clear pictures of her fantasy. Their closeness and his receptive state had created a remarkably clear, visual transmission. In the second incident, Jody was the "receiver" rather than the sender.

About five years into her marriage, Jody's husband, John, had an affair with a woman with whom he worked. Of course, he denied any romantic involvement with the woman yet he kept talking about her and their "business lunches" together. Being very sensitive to his thoughts and moods, Jody grew more and more suspicious. These suspicions grew as the number of his late nights "at work" increased, and as he grew cold and sexually disinterested in her. They had always had a very intense sexual relationship. She accused him. He denied it, telling her that it was her imagination. She began to question her sanity.

One evening after Jody had gone out to visit a friend, John went out. He refused to say where he had been. Jody did not think that he had gone to see the woman because he had mentioned that her sister was visiting her. The next morning, after John left for work, Jody sat in bed thinking about where he might have gone. She felt desperate to know, anxious yet determined to end the tension. She closed her eyes and a picture formed. She saw a sparsely furnished living room. Two women sat on a sofa, close together. One had her arm about the other's shoulders and Jody felt that they were lovers. John sat in a chair with a scantily clad girl standing in front of him. The girl pulled John out of the chair and they went up the stairs together. Jody was sure that they were going to make love. The entire scenario seemed very real to her, more like a memory than a dream, but too incredibly strange to have happened.

A month after this incident, John confessed his affair with the woman at work. Jody demanded to know where he had gone that particular night for she was still haunted by her vision. He told her that he had driven to his lover's house where he had met her sister and her sister's lesbian lover. His lover was dressed in a black lingerie costume that she had worn for some cheesecake pictures that her sister had taken of her. They sat in the living room talking for a while, then she and John went upstairs together. Jody's vision was certainly not as incredible as she had thought.

What is the effect of such telepathy on relationships? A young, married woman, Debbie, came for a session with Gay. She was in a dilemma. She loved her husband but she had fallen in love with a woman. Her very identity was suddenly in question. She had begun an affair with the woman and her husband was aware of that. Both her husband and her lover were being extremely understanding as they waited for her to make a decision between them. After a brief discussion of the woman's beliefs about being forced to make a choice in relationships and lose, Gay addressed the immediate situation:

"You have drawn to you two individuals who, despite understanding from the mind, the intellect, I feel that each of them, at a deeper level, would like to be special with you and so I feel a deep psychic pulling from both directions. As I said, at one level they do understand, and they believe that they understand, but part of this understanding is to show you how understanding they are and yet, as I said, there is a pull and I see you taking care of them both in different ways."

Gay then went on to explain this "pull" in terms of past-life influences in which the three of them had participated in various "triangles," each one pulling at the other. Debbie was relieved by the idea that her indecision and inner conflict was not all her own. Here she had been surrounded by these two "understanding" people who both claimed to love her very much and want only what she wanted. Now she could begin to stop feeling like the only "crazy" one, the only "selfish, indecisive" one in the situation. She was being pressured mentally and once she could sort that out, she might begin to know what she wanted.

The effects of telepathy are subtle and usually denied in our Western culture, with its materialistic (rather than spiritual) view of reality. As we begin learning to acknowledge their existence and examine the ways they affect our lives, we find that we can have more choice in how we create our lives. Sometimes our very basic beliefs about ourselves are affected by the thoughts, feelings, and judgments of those around us, especially those who love us. Debbie's self-image had been strongly influenced by the outward "understanding" of her lover and her husband. She believed that she was the only confused and conflicted one, that she was the only one that had a vested interest in what was happening. Gay's simple words about "psychic pulling" helped bring into focus a deeper drama that was occurring below the surface.

Sandy's relationship with Len gave her an opportunity, over the years, to learn how this telepathy affected her and, consequently, others with whom she now works. From the very beginning of this years-long relationship, she would feel confused, with painful thoughts often entering her mind uninvited, thoughts which would call into question her self-esteem, her worth. Certainly these were issues that she was working through during those early years with Len. Because they were important issues for her to confront, the effects of Len's influence were undeniably helpful in bringing her to the necessary confrontations. Part of her learning, however, as she built her self-esteem and developed a sense of her own worthiness, involved learning how to separate her feelings and thoughts from his. Shortly after she and Sheila began communicating with Gay Bonner, Gay began stressing the importance of this kind of separation in relationships.

Early in 1979, she laid out a basic premise that Sandy fought but later had to accept as true. All during her early years with this man, she suffered tremendous swings in mood and thought, one moment she was sure of his love and extremely happy with their interaction, the next moment, she was feeling as if he did not even care and fantasized about how he was going to hurt her next. And often he did by withdrawing his physical presence or his emotional self, distancing her with hints of other women or threats that he would leave the area. After a particularly intense period on this emotional see-saw, Gay told her:

"His energy is strong around you and you are choosing to open to these energies and to alleviate his suffering psychically for him. This is your choice. See it as a choice, realizing, however, that you are not helping him by doing this. You can help both of you by freeing yourself. The way to do this is to say "no." "No" is very difficult now for you to say to him but it is very important to begin to believe that you can be free. You still do not believe that you are allowed freedom and the feeling of peace that comes with this psychic freedom. You are absorbing his guilt, and the guilt is causing torment in you. Deep inside, you believe that if he realizes how you are suffering for him, he will be back. This is why you do this. At a psychic level, he is aware of this and he alternately likes it and resents it. Don't judge yourself, for you do want this man. He wants you as well, but until one of you decides to free yourself, there are struggles and turmoil. The relationship had been going well and now it is not. That is simply a switch that gets turned off and on and you participate in that as well. You need time for creative pursuits, and when it is good with him, you do not allow yourself other things, and then you also resent this."

In these words, Gay laid out a plan for learning that Sandy was to take several years to work through. She did not even understand what Gay meant when she said that Sandy needed to say "no." It seemed to her at the time that Len never asked her for anything. For her, the beginning of awareness began a few days later when she realized that saying "no" meant asking for what she wanted instead of always trying to please him by guessing what he might want. Learning not always to take on his feelings and attitudes was a much longer process. However, learning how he acted out behavior for her took even longer to grasp.

A couple of years later, Gay again brought up the issue of "choosing" to share his moods. Sandy had awakened one morning feeling depressed and filled with what she called "paranoia." She wrote in her journal: "I seem to go along fine mentally for weeks then a bout of paranoia hits. I don't know why this happens. Nothing has triggered me, at least nothing I'm conscious of. Certainly no event on the physical plane has occurred, yet I awoke this morning filled with apprehension, my mind creating one fantasy after the other in which I am hurt in some way. I focus it all on Len, of course." Frustrated, she decided it was again time to consult Gay.

"Sandy, you have consciously and unconsciously chosen to be open to Len and, in a way, you have asked to share his moods and feelings and so you do, as you did this morning. It is how you share, among other ways, of course. What you need to accept is that perhaps you will never know "for sure" that is so, but it is. Simply continue to send him love and realize this is part of your sharing. You do not necessarily have a problem. You have known for many years that his feelings are not dealt with consciously and you have even had "proof" of this."

Here was the same message. Sandy "chose" to take on Len's thoughts, feelings, and moods. Sandy did know that Len often did not express his feelings directly but would hold them in, eventually becoming depressed and moody. As the years went on, Sandy began to trust what Gay had been telling her. Recently, during the writing of these pages, she again awoke one morning with a feeling of depression. Nothing in her external life warranted these feelings. That evening, she called Len, asking how he was feeling. "I've been depressed all day," he complained.

Sandy did finally learn to separate her feelings from his, giving herself a choice as to whether or not she would "take his feelings on" as her own. She has not lost the ability to know what he is feeling at any given time, but she does now have more choice about what she feels or thinks about herself.

The effects of telepathy, however, have even more far-reaching consequences. Often over the years, Len has been able to influence Sandy's behavior, altering choices that Sandy would make in her life. Sandy or Len, it mattered little which one, would decide to end the relationship.

Sandy would usually become very angry with what she perceived as his withholding and announce to him, and all of her friends, that she was "through," that the relationship was ended and she was getting on with her life. Len's version was to simply withdraw, making himself completely unavailable to her, refusing to take her calls or return them. Weeks would go by and Sandy would go through the pain of letting go, making plans to go on with her life, sometimes opening to new men whom she would start dating.

Usually about three months into such a separation, she would begin to feel psychic pressure. She would find herself fantasizing about Len, forgetting all of the pain and remembering the pleasure. She would shake herself and attempt to block out these thoughts, concentrating on what she was trying to build in her life, her work or a new relationship. Then the dreams would begin. First, Len would simply appear in her dreams, his presence distant and peripheral to the dream events. This would happen several times a week for a while. Then Len would figure more prominently in the dreams, usually in a hostile role, criticizing her or turning away from her, often going off with another woman. Eventually, the dreams would shift tone, and Len would be acting toward her as if he were still her lover and everything was fine between them. She would awaken feeling loved and wanted and the fantasies would increase. At that point, something would happen on the physical plane. He would call or she would, finding him delighted to hear from her, anxious to return her calls. Sometimes she would hear from a mutual friend that he missed her but was afraid to call, assuming that she was still angry. By this time, all anger was forgotten and she would rush to the phone.

This pattern occurred several times before she finally recognized it. When she did, she went back through her dream journals and found the recorded dreams. Again, the questions would always arise in her. Was it all her doing? Her own wishful thinking? Or did he contribute to the pattern? The evidence pointed toward the latter. He often was the one to call first. He was always glad to hear from her and anxious to see her. Once that happened, he and she often fell back into their old ways of relating and not much would change. She would complain of his withdrawing and he would say that she asked for too much. She was constantly frustrated with it all, always wishing that she could be free of him to open to a more viable relationship. The bond, however, was deep and achieving that separation was difficult.

The year before these pages were written, Sandy and Len went through a rather dramatic illustration of how telepathically linked they are. Sandy had broken off the relationship early in the year. She had reached her goals in terms of her work and was now easily using her creative abilities in that area of her life. Consequently, this time she was determined to achieve separation from him and draw into her life a workable love relationship. She allowed six months to go by before even considering that she might meet someone else. Then she did. She was delighted with Charlie. He seemed to be everything that she wanted in a relationship. He was attractive, intelligent, creative, and interested in her psychic and spiritual work. The only drawback that she could see was that he lived at least two hours' driving time from her. The day that they met, they had instant rapport and made plans to see each other again soon. Three days later, Len called for the first time in six months. Sandy could feel herself freeze. She did not return his call. Several weeks went by and she did not hear from Charlie. She could sense that Len's energy was keeping him away but when that thought would enter her head, she would tell herself that that was ridiculous, that she was being melodramatic. After several weeks, and a couple of unreturned calls from Len, Sandy decided to take a step.

She wrote Charlie a note suggesting that they meet near his hometown for a drink. She was going there for a conference so it was a convenient solution. He called her immediately and said that he would definitely meet her; that, indeed, he had been "going to" give her a call and had even thought of sending her flowers but that "something" kept getting in the way of him taking that action. He had had some family difficulties which were his explanation for the delay.

They met and had a wonderful time. She was in the area for four days and three nights and they spent as much time together as was possible. Sandy felt that she was falling in love. It was exciting. Years had passed since she had felt that possibility. He was attentive, caring, and seemed absolutely delighted to have her in his life. She left him feeling that she had finally made an important change in her life. That feeling did not last.

Driving home, as she was passing through Philadelphia, thoughts of Len intruded into her consciousness. These thoughts increased with intensity as she approached home and she "knew" that he had called. The thoughts were insistent and she began making comparisons between Charlie and Len. She knew that this kind of indulgence was dangerous and ridiculous. She got angry. By the time she walked into her front door, she was seething. She went right to her answering machine and listened for messages. There were many but none from Len. She breathed a sigh of relief and told herself that she was being "crazy." Then she went upstairs to her bedroom and there, next to the bedroom phone, was a message from the woman who had stayed with her son during her absence. "Len called. Please call him back."

Furious, she did. Usually she would not dump her psychic revelations on him because he was not open to such interpretation of reality but this time she was beyond caring. She yelled at him that she wanted him out of her life or in it but that she was tired of the see-saw (a recurring and often repeated complaint). She then went on, probably quite incomprehensively to him, about this "phone call coming at the wrong time as always." He typically drew back and said that he could not deal with what has happening and would call her later.

He did call back two days later acting as if nothing had happened. He asked her for a date. She could not believe that! Laughing by this time, she agreed to see him in two weeks. She had a date with Charlie the following weekend, and made plans to spend Thanksgiving with him. She figured that by the time she had seen Len, she would be able to tell him that it was over. That is not what happened.

Charlie came for the weekend and Sandy found that she simply did not want to be with him. Suddenly everything was wrong and she knew that she was not in love and that this man was not for her. She was relieved when he cancelled the Thanksgiving Day plans because of family obligations. He sent a huge bouquet of flowers in his place and she resented the gesture. By the time she saw Len the following Saturday she was ready to open to him.

Outwardly none of this makes sense. It sounds like a soap opera, one of poor quality at that, but this pattern had gone on for years. As much as Sandy had learned about herself and the influence of Len's thoughts on her moods and behavior, she was still affected by it. She could not be sure whether she really did not want Charlie or whether Len's presence in her life again shut Charlie out of hers. She had found herself suddenly thinking critically of Charlie, finding many reasons why he wasn't for her. Len explained his reentry into her life at this particular point by simply insisting that he began to miss her terribly and acted on it. Certainly he was not consciously aware that she had met a new man. He did seem, however, to "know" that on some level and that "knowing" perhaps brought about the feelings of missing her and the subsequent action. Her angry response to this was exacerbated by similar past experiences. This was not the first time over the years that she had been with someone new and Len had suddenly come toward her as if he could not live without her. Her frustration would later increase as he again became secure with her only to once again withdraw, apparently when he realized that he really did need her. Her problem was clear. She still let him get away with it, in effect, she was still not saying "no" to him.

A discussion of the effects of telepathy in this relationship would not be complete without mention of two common phenomena—psychic storming and psychic "attacks." Sandy described psychic storming in *Being Alive Is Being Psychic:*

"Everything seemed to go crazy! She [Sandy] lost her address book. She lost one hundred dollars of Mind Matters money. The windshield wipers on her car kept going on and off for no reason. She kept hurting herself, not seriously, just bumps, bruises and little cuts. Nothing on her job worked out well, papers were lost, appointments broken, people unavailable. She wondered what in the world was going on! Then she heard that the man she was "storming" with was experiencing similar events in his life. He had broken his glasses. His car was not working. His job was going badly. He continually complained that the whole world was coming apart! Sandy asked Gay what was going on.

"That man is influencing you more than you want to see. Angry thoughts create an atmosphere like a storm when they meet each other. Be calm, peaceful. These are two people creating angry thoughts which meet and cause this unrest and create the trouble-some situations."

This event involved Len. At the time, they were not seeing one another at all and had no contact. Sandy learned of his distress from a mutual friend who did not know of their intense relationship. This friend, hearing Sandy complain about all of her current difficulties, remarked, "That's really odd! Len is going through similar difficulties." It was at that point that she had asked Gay about the situation.

Five or so years later, Gay again referred to this "psychic storming" between them. He had again withdrawn from her during one of their cyclical patterns, and she was experiencing the same sort of "difficulties" described above. She was also quite sure that he too was experiencing these kind of incidents. Gay confirmed that:

"You are punishing yourself for wanting to be free and you are, in a sense, creating these storms in order to give yourself difficulties. I feel that Len truly is not wanting to be close or committed but, as you know, at deep levels he already is and so he is troubled on the spirit level. You feel responsible for his happiness and sometimes that responsibility causes you to do things that hurt your-self. You are afraid to turn your back totally on him. Always he has known that he did not need to do anything and you would be there. He has been realizing that this may no longer be so and is fighting to keep things as they were. Naturally the battle is manifesting on the physical plane. Interestingly he too is having many, shall we say, mini-crises—many small accidents and problems."

And there it was again. A few days later, addressing this issue in Sandy's life and a completely different issue in a friend's life, Gay carried the concept of psychic storming even further. Sandy's friend, whom we will call Karen, had received a scathing letter from her older sister. She had always been close to this sister and was devastated by the letter which attacked Karen's attempts to expand her psychic and creative abilities. Gay began with a reminder:

"This is something you have heard many times but I must emphasize it. You can only be responsible for your own feelings. You have only this responsibility. You are not responsible for the reactions of others. You can listen but do not accept blame. Self-acceptance is important. You, Karen, received a written form of the same feelings that Sandy is being assaulted by and so you are in a similar position. It is just not so obvious in Sandy's case. Of course, she realizes what is not obvious because she accepts the mind as real and the message is communicated clearly through the mind.

"In both instances, you need to recognize a psychic attack. Do not misunderstand "attack." I am not saying it in a derogatory manner. It does exist, however, and you need to recognize it. Attacks are quite common. You do it yourselves and you have done it to these individuals involved. It is like a circle back and forth. All you can do is end your attack. This may seem difficult but not for you because you recognize your feelings. Recognize that you do not need to keep these feelings as your defense. You need no defense because you have done nothing wrong. See yourselves as deserving to be free. Your experiences are being attacked by someone who is jealous of your freedom.

"In your case, Sandy, the freedom does not seem so obvious but you have much more freedom than you recognize. You have hidden your freedom in order to help him with his feelings. Your freedom, Karen, is more obvious but your sister does not recognize your equal feelings of being stuck. To you the freedom is worthless because you are immersed in guilt. Sandy, you are learning not to limit your freedom even when you think of your potentials. However, then comes the guilt."

The concept of psychic attacks has often been explained in psychic and occult literature. Usually these attacks are seen as deliberate rituals performed by individuals who wish harm upon another. Voodoo dolls are an example of such ritualistic activities. Gay's definition widens the concept and shows that every one of us is capable of such interaction without even realizing it. Her in-depth explanation of the feelings that Karen and Sandy were dealing with—the angry responses and the guilt—show how easily we can indulge in "warring" with another, sending out thoughts and emotions which can potentially affect another.

Important also, however, is her initial warning. "You can only be responsible for your own feelings." By accepting that responsibility, then we can each make the choice as to whether or not we will participate in such a war. If we recognize our own anger or guilt or fear, we can then find ways to express those feelings cleanly, freeing ourselves from the battle. The only way to win such a war is to disengage from the fighting. This means taking deliberate action to redirect our thoughts in positive directions and to accept and handle our own emotions.

In intense sexual relationships, there is often ambivalence about what is wanted in the relationship within both people. That ambivalence is often acted out in psychically agreed upon patterns and roles. The awareness of telepathy in such situations is of utmost value. It allows individuals to free themselves from the emotional and psychic traps that interfere with our efforts to grow toward a conscious creating of our reality. Awareness of how the thoughts of others affect us also enriches our communication efforts as we realize that we have the ability to relate to one another on many levels.

Chapter IX

Relationships as Learning Grounds: Beliefs

"You *believe* that love means pain." As Gay's words penetrated Sandy's consciousness, years of learning to be self-aware began to fall into place. Yes, that was absolutely correct. She did believe that love means pain and had "always" believed that. She had believed it so thoroughly that, for her, it was an indisputable fact that she supported with concrete evidence from the events of her life. Now, for the first time, she began to realize that this was simply a belief that she held. A new perspective arose as a wave rippling out from her center, singing the possibility of new, viable relationships that resonate with a joyful tone rather than painful crying. Insight poured into her, connecting many pieces of learning throughout the years. Gay's words had followed information concerning Sandy's relationship to her mother, how she and her mother had struggled in past lives, creating anger and guilt that led Sandy to believe that she deserved to be punished, to suffer. "Then the belief extends to other intimate relationships and you believe that all love means pain," Gay concluded.

Many years before, Sandy's therapist had suggested that her difficulties in relationships with men lay with her mother. Sandy had thought that the therapist was crazy. This learning had now come full circle and everything began falling into place for her. She realized that all of her relationships, particularly with men, had been there as material for her to use to learn, in this particular moment, that she had a belief that was limiting her, keeping her from creating joy in her life.

What is this all about? We come into this physical life on this particular planet and here we engage in all manner of interactions with each other, with nature, with ourselves, and with our work and our play. Is it possible that it is all much easier than we might have dreamed? We struggle in our search for acceptance, love, success, or whatever we have set for our goal. Certainly in the "battleground" of sexual relationships, we have created eons of struggle that have lead to cultural beliefs so engrained in our psyches that we insist that they are facts. How many of us believe that "love means pain?" Any one day of listening to the popular songs on our radio stations will illustrate how pervasive that belief is throughout our culture. And it is only a belief. As a belief, it can be changed, consequently changing our reality, for our beliefs are the building blocks of our reality. We get what we think, and we think what we believe, and we then turn to our self-created reality to prove that we are right. There is no better place to begin unlearning such a cycle than the area of relationships. The next three chapters will deal with relationships as learning grounds for personal growth, a growth toward the direction of our birthright, a joyful physical existence on a rich and beautiful planet with others like ourselves who, if allowed, can contribute to our personal joy.

For Sandy, the belief that "love means pain" was an intensely personal one, tied up in lifetimes of believing that she was too bad a person to deserve anything other than punishment in relation to others. Such a belief becomes cultural when enough people believe it, and it begins to permeate popular expressions of their culture—music, movies, theater and so on.

Peg is a quiet, soft spoken woman who has consulted with Gay several times over the years. During one of her first sessions, prompted by the end of a rather intense relationship, Gay opened her statement with the following:

"It is only your beliefs and thoughts about doing what you want to do that rule out being close to someone else. Unfortunately, many individuals assume that to be close, you must give up your own individual goals and ideals. You must have agreement on direction in life. This is not necessarily so but believing this makes it so."

At the time, Gay's generalization about "many individuals" seemed to pass by Peg's awareness. She was devastated by the end of her relationship and when Gay later suggested that "I am not sure you did not want this to happen (the end of the relationship) so that you could be free to pursue other interests," Peg insisted that that certainly was not true. She wanted the relationship. She was sure. She soon had a new affair with a medical doctor. This doctor had many plans for her and encouraged her to go to medical school. Peg came to see Sheila and Sandy once again, expressing her doubts about her ability to keep up with the strict scientific requirements of such a venture.

Sandy asked her what she wanted to do. "Oh, it sounds like a wonderful idea and Bob would be so pleased." She started school. After several semesters of struggle, she finally gave it up. Her relationship with Bob continued for a few more years during which time she found that she could be quite successful in business. As her success grew, the relationship faltered. Bob, it seems, was jealous of her success. He wanted her home and available to him. She loved her job and refused to quit. The conflict ended the relationship. She had drawn someone into her life who fulfilled the belief that she "must give up" her own individual goals and ideals and have "agreement on direction in life."

For Peg, as it was with Sandy, this belief was tied to her self-image. She did not believe that she deserved to have a close relationship unless she was willing to give up her own desires. Gay had said to her after the end of the first relationship mentioned above:

"No influence is destined to continue to affect you and becoming aware of influences is a step in helping you to let go and become free. You can have everything that you want, perhaps not with the particular people you focus energy on but as long as you do not feel worthy of having everything, you continue to focus in directions that enable the original premise about yourself to remain true. You must simply reflect upon what you want, not any particular individual, but the qualities you desire such as freedom and intimacy together."

It took Peg several more years of trying before she would begin to finish the learning that Gay laid out for her. Beliefs about self-worth and, what Sandy has come to call "deserving issues," are, more often than not, the underlying limitations that we humans use to keep ourselves from fulfilling relationships and satisfying, creative work. Somehow, early in life, we learn from a variety of cultural, religious, and parental influences that we are unworthy, not good enough, or that we must constantly struggle to "earn" love and acceptance by getting good grades, pleasing others, being a "good" girl or a "nice" boy, choosing the "right" profession or spouse, whatever we believe is expected of us in order to "make it right" so we can be happy. As we begin to learn that these very personal beliefs about ourselves are simply beliefs that we have accumulated throughout our lifetimes, we can begin to let go and open to the possibility that we can, indeed, "have everything." We can begin to believe that we are okay as we are and we do not have to do anything in order for that to be true.

Right action in the world comes out of a sense of our own worthiness. When we believe that we deserve love, acceptance, abundance, creative expression, freedom to be who we are, and so on, we let go of trying to manipulate the world into giving us that which we believe we can not have. We let go of destructive, manipulative, jealous, prejudicial, even criminal, behaviors and attitudes. Our personal challenge then, in our present lifetime, is to become aware of what we believe about ourselves and recognize that we have the power to change what we believe, letting go of limitations and opening to a greater creativity.

Beliefs about self-worth are personal beliefs; they are what we believe to be true about ourselves. Often such personal beliefs dictate how we are "supposed to be." A man who is afraid of expressing his emotions, for instance, may believe that any emotional "display" leads to loss of control. He may perceive such expression as "woman's domain." Often such men attract women who take on the responsibility of expressing all the feelings within the relationship. Ted was such a man. He and his wife had had a "contract," according to Gay, in which she was responsible for his emotional life and he, in return, was the economic provider. When Ted's wife began chafing under this limited contract and moving out into the world seeking her own creative work, he became extremely distressed. He came and talked to Gay. She stressed his need to "let go," describing what she meant by that specifically for him:

"Letting go for you involves giving yourself permission to feel your emotions. This is something very frightening, for you associate anger with physical violence. This is not necessarily how it needs to be, but this is a result of your past lives. I also feel that, in your present life, you saw anger acted out in a very violent way. This frightened you and you resolved to be more sane than that. "

Ted's experience had led him to believe that he was "supposed to be sane" and that meant not expressing his emotions. To do so meant possible violence. His wife was growing tired of being the one who always acted out the feelings within the relationship. She wanted a more balanced interaction. Gay continued:

"If each of you is willing to be responsible for your own emotions,then there will be no blame or guilt. These two, blame and guilt, do not help to bring you closer. They add distance. Anger is not the same as blame. You can be angry and simply allow yourself to feel this emotion. It will not need to lead to violence."

In Ted's mind, anger *always* leads to violence which was "crazy" so he had to deny feeling anger in order to be "sane." Denying one emotion usually leads to denying all emotions and so he came to believe that he was supposed to be a certain way. As his wife changed her former belief that in order to have intimacy she must please her husband, he was forced to examine his own self-image.

Another personal belief that interferes with healthy relationships has to do with power. Sandy calls this the "I cannot" syndrome. People who believe that they are completely powerlessness in the world will often draw to themselves relationships that confirm that belief. Most often, in our culture, these people are women who become the abused victims who enter crisis shelters, having been physically beaten and/or mentally defeated. They believe that they are worthless, and that they have no power over what happens to them. They are often complainers who can spend hours describing how badly they have been treated and how terrible their partners are. Then they return to those same partners or draw similar ones over and over. Learning to take personal power and subsequent responsibility for creating one's reality is often a long process for these people.

Sandy knew a man who fit this pattern, proving that it is not always a "female" problem. Jerry was an attractive, sensitive young man who had married early and engendered a daughter. The woman he married soon began sleeping with other men. He began to drink. The alcohol increased his self-loathing and opened him to further abuse from his wife. They separated. Because of the daughter, the relationship continued and the abuse intensified. The mother gained much weight and soon physically overpowered Jerry as much as she previously had overpowered him mentally. She beat the child and when Jerry stepped in to stop her, she turned on him, physically beating him. He then withdrew from his daughter leaving her to the vagaries of her mother, increasing his guilt and sense of powerlessness. He drew other women into his life who either betrayed him or treated him as a helpless child, thereby keeping him weak. He viewed the world as a hostile place which was always trying to hurt him.

When his daughter became a teenager, she ran away from her mother. She had, in fact, attempted this a couple of times, running to Jerry. Each time, Jerry returned her to her mother. He was afraid of his ex-wife or of the woman with whom he presently lived. This final time, the daughter managed to manifest a viable foster home where she was loved and could learn about her own worth. Jerry recognized her strength and, for the first time, rallied his own. He took a stand and helped his daughter gain the legal means to establish her new life. In doing so, he had to stand up to his former wife. His sense of personal power surged and Sandy predicted positive changes for him in the future. Often, to counter a life-long belief about ourselves, we need to take some kind of action on the physical plane that contradicts the belief, thus learning that the belief is not necessarily true.

In addition to the variety of personal beliefs about ourselves that we create in order to learn, we also hold many beliefs about "the nature of things." These beliefs may not dictate how we feel we are or should be, but rather shape our perceptions of the world in such a way that we constantly limit that which we allow ourselves to enjoy. One such belief that both Sandy and Sheila struggled with through the years had to do with the nature of commitment. Commitment was struggle, giving up of something, a loss of freedom, identification with another person and everything that person represented, loss of individual identity, squelching of creative expression, and so on. In her relationship with Len, Sandy would swing between insisting that *she* was ready for commitment and Len avoided it, and knowing that she was scared to death of living with him or any other man because she "knew" she would no longer be able to be who she was.

In *Being Alive Is Being Psychic,* Sandy quotes a lecture that Gay delivered to her regarding her relationship to Len:

"Actually you humans on a physical level do not understand commitment. Commitment is not something you decide. It is not even static or fixed or permanent. It is or is not. You are both already committed anyway. The bond is there, and there are no big decisions to make. The fear is in admitting that you are committed now. Saying this for you both implies that it is forever and chains are around you. You both believe because of past experiences, that it will mean unhappiness and dishonesty. It need not mean chains, unhappiness, or loss of freedom. It can be liberating, but it is up to you. I am not predicting anything but only explaining commitment. Commitment is not a promise, a vow. It is a psychic bond and simply exists or does not. When it does not, you will both know and be ready for new experiences. When it does, simply enjoy and love. Very simple." (Pages 16-17)

Gay delivered those words to Sandy in 1979. She is still working through those very deep beliefs about the nature of commitment.

Dale likes beautiful women. In fact, he will not date a woman who is not physically beautiful. He has had many relationships with these women over the years and yet has not found "the one woman" whom he insists that he desires for a long-term commitment. His complaints about these relationships usually bemoaned the "fact" that the woman was not what she "appeared" to be and so betrayed him in some way. As a long-time friend of Sandy and Sheila's from California, he would often write to them with questions for Gay. Often these questions would concern his dreams, for he had discovered that his dreams were his door to psychic awareness. Not only would he find that the dreams were often prophetic, but they would also reveal his limiting beliefs. On one occasion, he wrote: "I have had several dreams telling me that I am drawing or will draw a woman to me who is unfaithful by her nature. I think that I believe that pretty women have more tendencies in this area because men find them more appealing and induce temptation with greater frequency."

Gay discusses how his belief about the "nature" of beautiful women creates this aspect of his life:

"You need to gain a new perspective about your relationships. Do not settle for less than what you truly want. I feel that your belief that beautiful women are "unfaithful" leads you to draw such women, and if a woman is not this way, you will set out to make her fit your belief. You would rather continue your painful experiences than change your belief system. I suggest that you look at the concept of being unfaithful and see if you are unnecessarily causing your pain because of your attention to surface behavior rather than deeper emotions of love. The behavior, sexually, of your partner often does not indicate diminishing love, only you have not learned to separate the two.

"Begin by realizing you do want faithfulness in whatever way that means to you and believe also that you deserve to have what you want. Later perhaps you might go the step beyond that I suggested, but for now picture in your mind what you want and see how your expectations create the opportunity. A deep part of you wants to feel victimized and believes that beautiful women are cruel and will hurt you. At this very deep level, you are angry with women and when they behave as you predict, you punish them by your own withdrawal."

And so by clinging to a belief about the "nature" of women, Dale was able to enact a continuing drama that reflected his own unresolved anger. Because beautiful women were "by nature" unfaithful, they would continue to hurt him so that he could punish them by withdrawing. Dale's dream had pointed in the direction of the surface belief in order that he might delve deeper into his feelings about women. Gay advised him to "see that love can be expressed in many ways and that particular actions do not indicate that you lack love from these individuals. You may need to allow yourself to feel love from other women who might not be what you would think of immediately as physically beautiful or desirable. Remember, you can have a beautiful faithful woman but, as I said, practice openness with all women and even all people in general."

Ironically, Dale's beautiful women had been expressing love by living up to his expectations. It was time now for him to let go of such limiting expectations and open to a greater possibility for himself.

Often, as was demonstrated with Peg earlier in this chapter, people's beliefs about the nature of "choice" in their lives leads them into interesting dilemmas. When beliefs about choice become "either-or" rather than the unlimited possibilities in a "and-both" approach, drama and subsequent learning can ensue. Margaret and Dan each create a different reality with the same core belief. Each was struggling with a need for intimacy and a need for freedom, each believing that the two were mutually exclusive. Dan's marriage was crumbling. He was distressed because he wanted the marriage. He had a three-year-old son who brought him much joy. His wife, however, objected to his traveling and his highly charged and creative work life. She wanted him home. He was a successful business man with endeavors in many parts of the country which constantly demanded his presence. Gay described the following belief structure:

"For you I have seen a life where you had to make choices, or thought you had to, between your freedom and your family. There has always been a call toward adventure but it has been painful. I feel that you have not trusted that you could still love and provide for those you loved. Rather you thought that you had to turn your back on them. Of course, you have drawn to you those who have been very traditional and unwilling often to explore the same areas as you, and so you had a belief that you had to make this very painful choice between intimacy and personal freedom. The need for freedom is very strong within you and you are protective of this. It is important to you and that is beautiful; however, you have often denied yourself opportunities to love and be intimate because you thought that the adventure would be gone from life. It is time to give yourself everything, to stop believing you must choose, believing you only have so much energy."

Margaret's struggle between intimacy and freedom took a different form. She was writing Gay to complain about the men in her life who had rejected her. One, her husband John, had divorced her. The other, Richard, a lover, refused to move to the South from the West coast in order to be with her. Gay refused to allow her to continue the perspective that these men had rejected her. She immediately jumped into Margaret's conflicting belief systems:

"You were taught that you would find happiness through using the intellect. Through the academic route you could find fulfillment. The other way you believed that you could find happiness was through relating to a man. It is these two belief systems that you are being made to examine, for you are asking for more from your life and so you have created your present situation. You have not been rejected by men. This is your interpretation, your perspective of what has happened. I feel it is important to change this perspective. Neither John nor Richard was what you needed from a relationship, and a deep part of your self accepted and understood this before you parted with either of these men. Your deeper self took part in structuring what was happening in these relationships.

"With John, you need to have more freedom to explore beyond the limited family. His view of the world was much too narrow for you. Although he was affectionate, you wanted more and so you also participated in ending the relationship with him. With Richard, I feel the opposite. He was more concerned with "freedom" than intimacy and a home environment and yet I feel you wanted more intimacy. You are attempting to find your own balance within, your own need for freedom versus your need for intimacy and so you chose and rejected the men who represented each. In your mind, you always had to choose between being close and being free. Being close represented being weak and dependent. Being free meant having no intimacy. You attempted both, shall we say, extremes and found them lacking. These men did not reject you. Rather, they each played their part in helping you see more clearly what you want and do not want. You are concentrating on the fact that they left, an appearance of rejection, rather than on the deeper truth."

Both Dan and Margaret deeply believed that they had to make a choice between two seemingly opposing ways of being in the world. They set up their worlds in order to begin the process of learning that they could have everything. Life could be approached with an attitude of "and/both" rather than "either/or."

Another common trap we create while learning in relationships is the belief that others must change in order for us to be happy. "If only he or she were different," is a frequently heard complaint. This age-old song rings throughout the history of relationships. Each of us can think of ways in which we act this one out. Sue wanted Doug to stop seeing other women and commit only to her. She struggled constantly with him in an attempt to get him to give her what she insisted that she wanted. While asking her questions of Gay, Sue concentrated on everything that was wrong with what he was doing to her. After giving her a history of past lives where they had often loved and separated, sometimes violently, Gay advised:

"I feel that you have been associated in several lifetimes and there have often been struggles, but that does not mean you need to continue to struggle. That is where your present creativity and new belief systems can change this. Now be advised that you might not wish to struggle anymore, and he may not be willing to change. In order for you to be with him without struggle, both of you must want to change. In order for you to find what you want in this life, however, he does not need to change. That is why the focus here is more on you than on Doug. And this is where your focus needs to be also. All you can do is decide for yourself."

In a different session, Gay spoke generally about how futile it is to attempt to control another's reality:

"Each reality is separate and unique, yet all work together to create the universe as you know it. It is wasting energy to attempt to change another's reality, although I also must say, there is not a waste of energy. The terminology is more for your benefit. It is futile, and therefore, seems like losing energy but upon giving up, you see all the energy there anyway. Actually it is simply another lesson in letting go. Reflect upon what you want in your relationships, not on any particular individual but on the qualities you desire in a relationship."

Often we believe that love means pain, that we must choose between opposing qualities, that others must change, that we don't deserve love, that beautiful women are unfaithful, or some other wonderfully complex belief. When we finally begin to learn that the events of our life reflect those beliefs and are there because we put them there in order to learn, we free ourselves to create and play with joy!

Chapter X

Relationships as Learning Grounds:
Patterns

"It is important for you to just be you and maintain your separateness. You are two sides of the same coin. He is struggling for separateness, knowing that he needs unity. You are struggling for unity, knowing that you need separateness. Just continue to be and know that if it is, it will be, and all is as it is because you need it to be as it is."

Gay was speaking to Sandy during the summer of 1978. The man that she mentions was someone in Sandy's life for an intense but short period that summer, a summer when she was not seeing Len. What is interesting here is that the pattern that Gay describes in this relationship was exactly the pattern that Sandy could see in her relationship with Len. As she thought about it, she realized that what Gay was describing was a common thread running throughout many of the relationship issues that people brought to Mind Matters. Most often, as in Sandy's case, the woman in the relationship was pushing for commitment, for intimacy, for sharing, especially of feelings. The man, as does Len, often withdraws, withholding his feelings, refusing to commit himself, even for the next weekend, certainly not for life.

As Gay's words penetrated Sandy's consciousness, she realized that her long struggle with Len (characterized by his withdrawal from her life during this very year, 1978), was indeed as she "needed it to be." She began then to understand that it was her need as much as his that perpetrated the see-saw effect in their relating. As with many women, Sandy saw herself as giving and nurturing. She did not want to think that she might be withholding. That was what Len would do. She could see that he needed "unity," that he shortchanged himself by giving little and receiving even less in terms of intimacy and closeness. It was much more difficult for her to admit that she needed "separateness." Over the years, she recognized more and more how true Gay's words were. She did need to keep herself apart from her lovers, particularly Len, for she was all too anxious to suppress her goals and desires in order to please him, to merge with him. She would often rail at him for what she called his "push/pull" behavior in the relationship. He would draw close to her, seeing her frequently, proclaiming his love and need for her. She would begin believing him, changing the goals and directions within her fantasies to include him, often letting go of those desires that she thought he would dislike or disapprove of. Then suddenly he would be gone. On the telephone he would be cold and distant, talking as if she did not matter in his life.

He would be "busy," unavailable to her. She would put herself through the pain of his withdrawal, feeling caught up short and deluded, having then to pull in her own fantasies, redirecting her life to exclude him. Often she would get some creative work done. She seldom saw that the work was getting done, however. For years, she focused on the pain that she believed that he was causing her.

Time, sometimes weeks, sometimes months, would pass and the pattern would shift. Len would return, usually enthusiastic about seeing her, feeling his need to be with her, to merge and be intimate. And off they would go again, repeating the same pattern. Sandy would complain, moaning about being stupid for "putting up with his inconsistent, inconsiderate behavior." And yet she did. Because of her tendencies to give away her own desires and goals in trade for intimacy, a very deep part of herself knew that she needed someone like Len in her life in order to do the creative work that she had laid out for herself. This knowing was not usually conscious, however. It took years before she realized her part in the pattern.

The intricacy of such contracts between people is so subtle that shifts in roles often occur, maintaining the form of the pattern while changing the roles of the principal characters. Just a few years ago, at a time Sandy was becoming more conscious of how this pattern played itself out between her and Len, she was amused to find the roles reversed. It was Christmas time and they had attended a party across town. Sandy was planning a trip to Florida over the holidays to visit her father. She planned to leave a few days before Christmas and return New Year's Eve or the day before that. She and Len usually attended a New Year's Eve party together. Most years, she would not know that they would actually be going until the last minute because he was always reluctant to make a commitment about any social engagement in advance. She was used to this behavior by now and did not get upset but simply waited it out. This year, because of her trip, there was more doubt about whether or not they would attend the party. Driving home from the Christmas party, a week or so before she was to leave, he brought up New Year's Eve. "Are you going to be home in time for Wade's party?"

"I don't know. I want to because Steven has to work."

"That's no reason for coming home early," he remarked. Of course, Sandy also had in mind the New Year's party but was reluctant to push him on it because of his past behavior. Suddenly, she heard him complaining.

"What will I do if you don't get home in time?" She was shocked. His petulant voice tone matched her feelings in past years when he refused to give her a definite answer about a social commitment. She savored the moment, turning to him and suggesting that he invite someone else or simply wait to see if she would return in time. She later realized that because of circumstances, their usual pattern of relating was reversed. He was acting out her role of the hurt, long-suffering, giving partner. She was being vague and withholding. Much of her resentment faded as she began to perceive the long-term pattern clearly. This event was one of many through the years that led to her "real" separation, a separation on psychic levels, making the physical separations and "see-sawing" unnecessary.

Most of us seem to have behavioral or thought patterns that we repeat throughout our lifetimes, hopefully learning as we go along. These patterns shift and change as we learn. One common metaphor often used in psychology is that of peeling an onion. Often we will lament when we find ourselves repeating something that we thought we had already learned, and then we realize that this particular event or situation is simply another peel of the onion, a little deeper and cleaner perhaps than the last, but still the same onion. As we work through the onion, we do find layers of influence—beliefs, parental injunctions, past-life experience, this-life experience, and so on. Sandy's belief that she must choose between intimacy and creativity is reflected in the pattern described above. Over the years, she discovered past-life situations that led her to her beliefs about the nature of reality in general and herself in particular. She could see that the people she drew into her life—her mother, Len, other lovers, even her own children—all conspired to force her to learn, to peel this particular onion in her consciousness.

During a frustrating time in the relationship in the early 1980s, Sandy consulted with trance-channel, Ginny Ramus, speaking to Valoos, who has a special connection to Sandy and often guides her when she feels the need. During this particular session, Valoos took Sandy several layers deeper into the onion. He described the learning in this relationship in soul terms rather than personality terms.

"The man, Len, I see popping in and out like threads through the tapestry of many lifetimes. Some frustration and conflict are there. In the larger relationship of souls which you two are at in any given time, you, Sandy, do feel in a variety of ways, various aspects of this larger relationship. Often, such as with the present set of circumstances, you use your intellectual resources to try to understand what is happening from the knowledge seemingly available to you. Any seemingly direct cause-and-effect set-up you may find will only have to be unraveled or unlearned, as later the deeper understanding does ease into your awareness."

Are you saying that our past lives are influencing this life now?

"Not as is caused by circumstances from other incarnations but rather the larger relationship between the larger souls containing several lifetimes each. This larger relationship is growing and developing and changing. As you know, each incarnation manifests various aspects. It is quite easy for you to understand from the larger point of view, but this understanding does not fit into the psychological terms and reasoning into which you are trying to fit an answer. Remember, the success of your relationship is not truly determined by lack of conflict or by pleasant times together, or even by your conscious intellectual understanding of one another. Please recognize too that you, Sandy, are one who likes to understand all that is happening within and without and this, of course, strongly includes people in your psychic and physical environment, those close to your heart. Len does not feel this way and becomes confused when things have to make sense to you. Much of his behavior in interactions with others, I see as not needing to make sense to him but as being motivated by seemingly random parts of himself. It is as though he were allowing energy in one part to be manifested experimentally for another part. On a larger scale, this occurs likewise with this being and sometimes you, who are sensitive to such occurrences, will notice a withdrawal of his energies or a strong flaring up of his energies at various times.

"You often interpret this as his withdrawal or coming toward you, not realizing that indeed this is more of his total energies than as the man, Len, and their interaction [the energies] in the life he is creating here. When energy is lower in Len's life, often it is higher in another incarnation of this being. Do you understand? (I think so but why am I with him and what am I learning from this?) Patience is one very large lesson here. The word patience is small but the concept enough to devote many lifetimes to, it is a major challenge for you in this lifetime. You are learning to put out and take in energy in ways most natural for you at any given moment. You and Len are drawn together by your love and do aid one another greatly in the development of yourselves. He learns much from you about loving himself, about being kind to himself. He had no idea before knowing you that he could let portions of himself shine through directly without being doctored and made up to present what he thought would be an acceptable image. You know his spirit, his soul, and are willing to put up with personality characteristics which are irrational and infuriating to your personality. You gain in the long run, as does he. Stay attuned to the love and know that this is where the nourishment comes from. Therein also lies the success of the relationship, and such success is beyond question."

Once again it was to take Sandy several years before the full implication of Valoos' words would lessen the frustration with the pattern existing between her and Len. However, she did realize that Len's withdrawal of energy was not so personal and stopped feeling that there was something wrong with her when he disappeared. The larger soul picture of their interaction did allow her to release some of her personality level judgments and hurts. Interestingly, Len would unwittingly confirm Valoos' words, reminding Sandy to keep the larger soul perspective. Many times he has said that Sandy "puts up with him when no one else would." He also talks about "not having enough energy." In fact, one of his most frequently spoken words is "energy," usually used in the context of relationships and social interactions.

As with Sandy, people often come into a particular lifetime in order to work out these patterns. One woman, whom we will call Carolyn, wrote to Sheila asking that Gay help her understand the confusion that she feels in her relationships with men. She was divorced and currently involved with a lover. She also asked about her "spiritual development." Gay told her that she had come into this life to "understand how to balance the physical and spiritual aspects of life." She then went into a rather lengthly explanation of how her spiritual development interrelated with her relationships:

"You are working in two different kinds of realities, or shall we say frequencies, and you are attempting to fit spiritual growth into a particular slot where things are done rationally and with the intellect. Your life, particularly your childhood, has been centered around developing the intellect and you have drawn people to you, particularly men, who reflect this idea that the intellect is to be worshipped above intuition, above the emotions. Your father was this kind of man and so are both your ex-husband and your current lover. This makes it very difficult for you, for you are much more attuned to the emotions and the inner self but heavily influenced by people in your life.

"You have in other lives often come close to doing psychic or spiritual kinds of work but were kept from this by husbands, lovers, or fathers. I see one life, for example, in the 17th Century New England, where you were being trained as a psychic's apprentice. The particular woman you were with, who happens to be your mother in this present existence, was accused of witchcraft and burned. You watched this happen. Your lover was one of the men involved in sentencing her to death. He was, of course, unaware of your activities. I feel that since you made the commitment to marry this man, you gave up your psychic activity and married him despite deep inner revulsion toward him. This man is now your ex-husband."

Carolyn's past-life situation is a dramatic mirror of her present life's conflict. She struggles to express her feelings and intuition only to be subtly put down and "corrected." Even with her current lover, whom she sees as a teacher and mentor, Gay suggested that she "look with a more critical eye. I do not mean negatively but with your eyes truly seeing rather than just looking. Each individual, of course, is unique and your lover and ex-husband are certainly unique, but I feel also a basic similarity in how they relate to you."

Carolyn's challenge then, in this lifetime, is to begin sorting out the various messages she receives from the men in her life from who she is and who she wants to be, balancing "the physical and spiritual aspects of life."

A very different kind of pattern was described in the session of a woman we will call Holly. Holly was an attractive, white woman who talked about a lifetime resentment of white men. All of her adult relationships were with black men. She had one male white friend named Rob. Gay described lives as black women sold into slavery in the early 18th and 19th Centuries. In the latter life, Rob was a white man who helped her escape. She was also a black musician in the early part of this century in San Francisco. There she met her present lover, who at that time, was her teacher and musical mentor. Then Gay described an even earlier lifetime with him:

"He had been your lover in Africa before you were forced to be apart. You were put on separate boats never to see each other again. This accounts too for some of your resentment and hate for white men. It is difficult for you to imagine them as kind. Even with your father in your present life, I sense some difficulty and resentment. This seems to be simply a part of your soul's memory bringing about the tendency to draw toward you men who were sometimes cruel and often angry. As I said, I see Rob as a helper.

"I feel this is a significant relationship in your life, perhaps leading you to seek help and continue to remain open as you go through changes. The changes involve letting go of these old influences and beginning to become free."

Holly was as much enslaved by her resentment and anger as she once had been by the men who captured her. Meeting one white man who was kind offers her the opportunity to let go of many lifetimes of physical and psychological slavery.

Learning to balance power within one's life is often worked out in the context of male/female relationships. Belle was a powerful woman on the edge of a potentially successful career. At the time of her session with Gay, she was in the process of making a decision to leave her husband and move to Europe to further her work. Gay talked to her at length about her goals and then about her marital relationship:

"I feel that you have been with Ben in many lifetimes and I feel that you met because he had something to teach you, something to show you about life. This you admired and yet you went beyond what he showed you, what he gave you, into your own kind of learning and awareness. I feel that the balance of power has shifted a few times throughout this relationship. There is at times a struggle for power here. That is happening now, a shifting, a need for you to feel your power. I feel in other lifetimes you have each been a parent to the other, so at times, particularly when you first met, this man seemed to be in control of things, much like you would think a parent would be. Then, at other times, I see you mothering him. It shifts back and forth. Now it is important for you to recognize in this relationship that you are seeking to balance this power."

This "shifting of the balance of power" between people in a relationship is a pattern. Early in the marriage, Ben had been the one who determined the direction of the relationship. The power had now shifted and Belle was the one in control. Ben was terrified that she might leave him and had been sending her strong psychic messages that he needed to be mothered. Gay's intent was to help Belle become aware of the dynamic operating between them so that she would be better able to make a clear decision for herself.

Another pattern in male/female relationships that demands attention is that of physical and psychological abuse, usually directed by the man toward the woman. We saw earlier (in Chapter 9) a situation where a man was physically abused by a woman. There the abuse was the result of his personal beliefs about himself and negative feelings of self-worth. The more common pattern, as is revealed daily in our newspapers, is the one of men beating their wives and lovers. Awareness of the psychic influences operating in these situations can offer the participants a depth of understanding that may lead to change.

Charlene was severely beaten by her boyfriend. She ended up in the hospital for a few days and suffered weeks of facial and body bruises. When she came to see Sandy and Sheila, she was wavering between going back to him or seeking revenge. Gay chose not to emphasize her role in the beating; however, both Sandy and Sheila felt that she probably had psychically drawn the event to herself. They had known her for several years and she was frequently in situations where she perceived herself as the victim who had been wronged by somebody whom she needed to fight. Gay subtly hints at this pattern then goes on to describe other influences:

"There is a recognition you must make that you do not need to suffer or have problems in order to have someone else care for you or to have someone relate intimately and closely to you. You have believed that you need to have a problem in order to relate to Richard and perhaps others, but for now we will focus on this relationship. The dramatic occurrences and arguments also add a fuel to your passion. Strange as this might sound, there is uncertainty here and a tension, and this has some excitement that interests you both. Richard is a very complex individual with many sides that he prefers to hide, from himself and certainly from others. I feel that there are secrets that he keeps both consciously and unconsciously. He does not want to feel that he is at any time out of control and so his usual behavior is to remain always, shall we say, cool and collected until pressure begins to build inside.

"There is a deep unconscious anger toward women and you from another existence where he took care of you. You were an invalid for many, many years. You were his wife and he felt obligated to stay with you. You had severe brain damage and you were paralyzed but he stayed. The resentment though was obvious, and you took on much guilt from this. I feel your desire at a psychic level was to help him through his own paralysis which was a paralysis of the spirit rather than of the physical body. I also feel, of course, learning and growth for you.

"I also see other lives as lovers and so you were, of course, drawn to him in this way. He had much resistance, for I feel also a mistrust of women in general. You were prepared to help him past this by being loyal no matter what, and now you are in a conflict. You are looking at two extreme alternatives, but you must find some balance. You could ignore this and go back with him, thus in your mind still showing him that he can trust women. Your other alternative or desire (quite naturally) is to strike back using whatever method you can, thus satisfying your need for revenge. Either direction is not desirable right now. Take more time and find the balance between the two. Do not, of course, neglect your own needs and feelings; yet remain open to this man's deep conflicts and emotions.

"You need protection of a psychic nature and perhaps some discipline to stay away for a while using meditation or a mental exercise to send him love. I do not feel that striking out in a physical way will benefit either of you at this time. You will be adding more anger and resentment to this relationship and perhaps setting up conditions for future meetings and relating in a future life-time. However, you need to look deeper into your own self and recognize where you feel you have been wronged by being the victim of an injustice. You, of course, feel your own anger, but acting solely from this emotion does not produce long-term peacefulness. You need to let go eventually and forgive, even though at first this seems distasteful, leaving you feeling vulnerable, perhaps weak. But you become more vulnerable by striking out or returning in your present state of mind. After you have accepted your own anger, focus on forgiveness and letting go. As difficult as it might seem, this is for yourself, not another. It builds inner strength and deep dignity. My suggestion now is one to help you avoid unnecessary struggles and to learn in an easier way. I do feel strongly that for a while you need to be away from this man."

Gay was, of course, pointing Charlene in the direction of awareness of the pattern that Sheila and Sandy had perceived as she told her story. It was a story that they had heard from her several times before. She drew men and situations into her life that ultimately placed her in the role of victim, powerless and angry, demanding revenge and believing that getting it was impossible. If she could let go of this dichotomy between powerlessness and revenge, she might be able to move into a sense of the peacefulness that comes with real personal power. The suggestion of forgiving, as Gay points out, is for her, not for the man who wronged her. Her real strength would come when she forgave and let go, leaving him caught short by not having a victim or force to fight, thereby possibly opening him to learn of his power as well. Her power would come not from capitulating or fighting, but from withdrawing her energy from the battle. She could then focus her energy on giving to herself in whatever way she chose. The past life information helped to give her a wider understanding of the context of the event and her ambivalent feelings afterward. This understanding laid the groundwork for the eventual forgiveness.

Sarah also had been a victim to men. She came to see Sandy at a point in her life where she was beginning to get herself out of this pattern. She was aware of her part in the pattern, had recently left her husband, and was participating in women's groups designed to increase awareness and find new resources. She was feeling quite strong about her new changes when she suddenly found herself in a situation which exaggerated all of her old behaviors.

Sarah is a school teacher. She has a ten-year-old son. During the school year, she had become attracted to a thirteen-year-old boy who was having difficulties at home. Sarah believed that this child had great potential as a human being but was caught in a negative home environment. She invited him to live with her and her son, thinking how beneficial it would be for her son to have an older boy around the house. For a few months, everything was fine. Then, at the beginning of the new school year, problems started. The boy, Mickey, started refusing to go to school. He acted out, insisting on having his way. When she objected, or attempted to parent him, he threatened her with violence. Her role as the adult in the house slipped quickly and she found him running her life. He gave her two black eyes. Her reaction to all of this was to hide. She lied to her co-workers and friends and protected him. She tried to get him to return to his family home but he would respond with threats to cut up her tires, burn down her house, and so on. She felt helpless and didn't know what to do. That was the point at which she came to see Sandy.

Sandy immediately saw that it was an issue of power and one that was probably rooted in past lives. She put Sarah in trance and suggested that she move into a past life that she shared with Mickey, if indeed such a life had happened. Sarah found herself cutting wood outside of a cabin in the woods. Her brother was inside the cabin. She was scared to go in. When she finally did, she found him drunk and pushing at her to drink with him. The feeling she had was that when he was around, he was always trying to make her do what she did not want to do. When he was away from the cabin, she lived in peace, working contentedly as a weaver. During this particular incident, he kept pushing at her to drink with him. She refused, they struggled, and he killed her with a broken bottle.

She was quite upset, but Sandy insisted that her spirit self remain near the physical body that she had just left. She watched what was happening below her, and saw the sheriff come and take him away. Sandy then suggested that her present self go to her past self in spirit form and talk to her. This communication was necessary so that they could help each other. The past-life self did not know how to protect herself. This was what Sarah was now learning. She had learned art and contentment from the past life self and realized how important it was that she learn to protect herself now, particularly from this man who had been her brother and was now the boy she knew as Mickey. In the spirit form, she could see that she had been in many lives with this entity, always acting out the same pattern. She became very determined to change this. Sandy led her through a psychic separation exercise with this man which her past-life self was encouraged to witness. Sandy also taught her how to use white light for psychic protection. Sarah felt much better and was now sure that she would know what to do on the physical plane.

Sometimes the woman who feels herself a victim is hiding her own fear of power in that role. Joan was just such a woman. She came to talk to Gay about her relationship with her husband of thirty years. She claimed that she was deathly afraid of him because she never knew what he might do. He yelled and screamed and occasionally would hit her. He behaved like a bully. She moaned and groaned, crying that there was nothing that she could do about it. Gay did not buy her drama:

"It is important for you to see how powerful you truly are. You are very strong and in many ways you are the powerful one in your house, but you are afraid of your strength, afraid that perhaps you could be violent. I feel that you would not be but there is a deep fear within you of losing control. Perhaps you also fear that losing control would be sinful and ruin chances for any kind of happiness. Allow yourself to be angry. Then your husband will not feel his own need to express all the anger. Give yourself permission to be strong. I feel he will not be as violent as you think if you truly begin to recognize your own power and remain firm."

Joan had a contract with her husband. She played helpless and he played bully. The truth was that she indeed held the cards. She had the power in the situation and could change the circumstances by simply owning her own feelings, particularly of anger. This pattern is common and not unlike the one of Sandy's described above where she was the warm, giving martyr and Len was the cold, withholding ingrate. Joan was afraid of her anger. Sandy was afraid of giving herself away. Both contributed toward the behavior of the men in their lives and needed to realize how they do this in order to regain their personal power and change their lives.

Kate was a woman who was determined to do just that. She came to see Sandy about a relationship with her boss. She could not understand what had happened in this relationship because it was so very different than the rest of her life. She came from a secure and happy family. She was still quite young but what relationships she had had with men were normal and stable and when or if a man treated her badly she would easily pull out and go along her happy way. Then came John. She had started working for him about seven months before this session. Soon after starting the job, they began dating. The relationship never became sexual because she soon realized that something wasn't right about his possessiveness and his constant subtle criticism of her. She broke off the dating. Her problem was that she couldn't bring herself to quit her job. She felt that he was holding her there. He continued to criticize her and undermine her usual confidence, making her feel that she had no ability or talent. Prior to this particular job, she had been quite successful in her field and had felt good about her work. Now she had doubts. She was afraid to look for another position. Intellectually, she knew that her boss was being unfair and acted from his own insecurities; however, emotionally, she felt stuck and could not bring herself to take the appropriate actions to free herself.

After questioning Kate for a long time, Sandy became convinced that Kate was relatively stable and secure in her sense of self. This particular situation seemed isolated and uncharacteristic. She suggested that they do a past-life regression.

At Sandy's command, the entranced Kate entered into another time and place where she had known John, her present boss. She found herself locked in a room, pregnant and scared. She knew that her husband was coming soon and was terrified because she had done something that she knew he would not like. He did come in and he did beat her. This turned out to be a recurring pattern throughout the entire lifetime and her marriage to the man she now knows as John. Sandy took her to her death. She died tired and alone. Taking the present Kate to her counterpart during the after death state, Sandy suggested that she communicate with that other self, comforting her but learning what she needed to know for her present existence. As Kate talked to her, it became quite apparent that Kate's distress in her present life was a call from the past-life self for help.

On the behavioral level, Kate had dealt with this man firmly and quickly, refusing to continue a personal relationship with him, and refusing to consciously capitulate to his criticisms and demands. She recognized, however, the feelings of her past-life self. She had felt those feelings during this relationship—the fear and the sense of self-defeat. What she needed to do now was convince the past-life self that it was all finished with him and she could let go of her stuck feelings. It took quite awhile for Kate to do this while in the trance but eventually the scared other-self heard her. She learned of Kate's strength which could now become her strength, and then symbolically moved toward the light. Kate felt an immediate sense of relief. She knew that she would now have no trouble finding a new job, and she did not.

There is one more pattern that needs to be explored here. Often people in relationship will attempt to become responsible for another's feelings. They become so concerned about how another might respond or feel that they limit their choices in order to keep the other from hurting or to make the other person happy. Unfortunately, this seldom works. Many, many times Gay has said to people, "The only happiness you are responsible for is your own. It is impossible to create happiness for another."

In our culture, we are often taught that we must not do or say anything that will "make another person upset." Thus we learn how to take responsibility for others' feelings. Len often does this with Sandy. He will guess how he thinks she will feel about something and then do everything he possibly can to prevent what he thinks might happen. This pattern causes much confusion and dissension between them because Len will pull away when he does not want to face what he thinks will happen. Sandy gets confused and frustrated.

A simple example of this occurred years ago when Len was planning a business trip to California. He asked Sandy if she would like to go. She, delighted, said yes. Later he thought about it and decided that he would be much too busy to properly entertain her. He then did not want her to go. Rather than discuss it with her, he withdrew from her. She was puzzled and angry because she did not know what happened. Finally he talked to a good friend who laughed at him and suggested that he tell Sandy how he felt. At first he was appalled by that idea because it would "hurt her feelings." The friend quickly pointed out that that was what was already happening. Len gathered up his courage and spoke to Sandy about his feelings. She was so relieved to find out that it was something so simple that she was glad to change her plans and go to California on her own a few weeks later. She found that Len had believed that he would be totally responsible for her well-being while they were there, just as he had felt responsible for her feelings about his decision. She did go to California by herself and visited all of the friends that she had intended to visit on the trip with him. This belief of his has often limited their social and recreational activities together and has been a difficult one to overcome.

While writing this chapter, Sandy had occasion to work with a young man caught in the same pattern. This young man was nineteen years old and in his second year of college. During his senior year of high school, he had dated a girl whom he had asked to the senior prom. She broke off the relationship with him a couple of months before the prom. He was hurt by her decision but weeks later, when she approached him to announce that she had bought her prom dress and was looking forward to the prom, he could not bring himself to tell her that he would now rather go with someone else. He was afraid to hurt her feelings even though she had been cavalier about his.

Now two years later, he had met a girl that he liked very much. He wanted an intimate relationship with her. Each time he tried to make love to her, he found himself impotent. This upset him terribly and was even puzzling because he had been sexually active for years with no problems. As he talked to Sandy, several issues became apparent. He did, indeed, like this girl more than any he had met over the years. He had plans for himself, however, that included changing colleges and leaving the area where she lived. She did not attend college but was a local girl who lived in a very conventional family with parents who had traditional expectations for their daughter. He found himself in conflict. He would talk to her about his plans to leave in order to further his education and experience and then imply that she would always be in his life. Two different parts were pulling on him, one part that liked her very much and one part had ambition and knew he would not be happy getting married at a young age and settling into a traditional lifestyle. Sandy pointed out the conflict and suggested that they do a trance session to seek a solution.

This young man has psychic abilities and has learned to work with psychic energies. It was in these abilities that he found his own solution. Sandy simply put him in trance, asked for the parts in conflict to be present, and then asked the higher self to negotiate a solution. She gave suggestions that if a past life was influencing the situation, he would know it. He listened to her suggestions and watched his own solution unfold. He "saw" the conflict and realized that he had indeed been pulled in two directions. Then as Sandy asked for the higher self to offer a solution, he saw a bright ball of light entering his head, moving down to the solar plexus where it burst into yet a larger ball of light, then quickly channeled up through his heart and out his throat.

Recently, in meditation, he had learned about the body's energy centers and had begun to perceive them visually. Now he saw them in action. Without intellectual knowledge of their meaning, he "knew" that what he needed to do was talk to the girl about his feelings. He had not done that because he did not want to "hurt her feelings" and he had not consciously been fully aware of his conflict. The light moving out through his throat told him that he needed to communicate with her and be very straightforward with her about his feelings and his plans. He came out of the trance relieved and pleased. He knew that this was an important lesson for him because of his pattern of wanting to take care of others' feelings. His body had been protecting him from what he feared—hurting her by his leaving. Now he felt that he would be able to have the intimacy he wanted with this girl and do what he knew he would be doing with his life. A solution that had been impossible for him to find on the intellectual plane offered itself to him on psychic levels. He needed to learn that he could not protect someone's feelings by holding himself back, that he could have what he wanted and give what he wanted to give if he was open and honest about his feelings. "If the relationship is to be a long-term one," he said to Sandy, "it will simply be that way. If not, we've enjoyed our time together." That simple statement could work for all of us if we could learn to be that clear.

It is important to recognize the patterns that repeat and repeat during our lives. We may seek a psychic solution, as did the young man, or simply learn the subtle influences contributing to the pattern. Either way, we can give ourselves more choice in how we create our reality if we learn to recognize and take responsibility for what we do.

Chapter XI

Relationships as Learning Grounds: HOW WE SET IT UP!

Gay was speaking to a group of people gathered with Sandy and Sheila to explore clarity in relationships. One of the participants asked her how we could be happier in relationships:

"First, relationships do not need improving as such. They exist as reflections of your own inner self. I suggest you do just what you are doing here—becoming clear about what you want. Focus on these particular qualities and will other thoughts to leave the mind. Do not worry about how these qualities will come about. Just trust that they automatically do. Your relationships now are reflections of what you are currently asking for. You already had certain programmed ideas about what you wanted and so this is what you have. As you change, your relationships can not help but change. In relationships you must realize there is no cause and effect. Just simultaneous interaction. You may not be aware of this, but your interactions are perfectly timed in rhythm and there is a pulse like music, rhythm, and even harmony (or what appears to be disharmony, but between the two it is actually always harmony.) It is music like instruments in a symphony orchestra. You only interact and you change as you interact. All happens simultaneously."

Later in the seminar, a man asked about his need to have a "primary" relationship with one woman. Gay's twist on the word "primary" led the group back to the point she was making above:

"This is difficult to answer because I see that all that exists is now. Either now you relate or now you do not relate and so I feel here must be your focus. Now. To me, "primary" implies other times than now. The time you live in is Now. For all of you, remember this too. You are relating or you are not. It is quite simple if you can stay in Now with the mind."

Sandy then cut in, asking, "Are you telling us not to go around making decisions about how things should be?"

"Well, you could make these decisions but they have very little value when the mind is attuned to Now and attuning to Now is the only way you achieve these things, so it is a paradox. I do not necessarily say do not make these decisions, but consciously attempting to decide these things most often results in more frustration. It is your choice to continue being frustrated and struggling, or to be in peace. All is simpler than you might think."

We human beings seem to have a propensity for making life much more complicated than it need be. Throughout the years, Gay has repeated that message over and over. We "think" ourselves into confusion, frustration, and pain. *"Become clear about what you want,"* Gay admonishes throughout these sessions. We always have what we have asked for in our lives, including our relationships. That is sometimes very difficult for most of us to accept. We moan and rage about the injustices perpetrated by others in our lives, forgetting that we are indeed the architects of our own reality. Learning how we set up all this frustration and pain is an important step toward letting it all go, so that we can live fuller and more satisfying lives with spontaneous and rich relationships.

There is no better place to observe the complexity we are capable of creating in relationships than the "eternal triangle." A theme throughout mythology and literature through the ages, the triangle demonstrates our inclination for creating frustration and pain. Sandy knows about triangles intimately having created a series of obviously patterned relationships over her younger years in which she played the role of "the other woman." As she moved into self-awareness, she had to begin taking responsibility for this pattern. Until then, she had always shrugged, declaring, "It's not my fault. It just seems to happen."

During her years in primal therapy in the mid-seventies, her therapist once suggested that her tendency to find herself involved with other women's men had nothing to do with the men. "It probably has to do with your mother," the therapist commented. Sandy was outraged at that idea and rejected it as "projection" from the therapist. What in the world would her mother have to do with any of this? Her mother did not seem to like men and, to Sandy's knowledge, had not been involved in any such relationships herself. Gradually, Sandy did learn about her mother's psychological influence on her, how indeed she might be striking out at her mother because of old hurts and anger, using these other women as surrogates for her mother. That idea never really felt real to her although she had to admit the logic of it. She was angry with her mother for many years. The pattern persisted, however, long after the anger dissipated. As she began to feel that she had more choice in the matter, she would shy away from potential married or committed lovers yet somehow they would appear in her life.

It wasn't until just a few years ago that Sandy was able to move through an experience that laid the pattern to rest. She had met a new couple she enjoyed being with. Soon there was an attraction between her and the husband. She was distressed about this and wanted simply to be friends with both husband and wife. During a session with Gay, she expressed her fear of setting up the same old pattern. Gay first gave her some information about her mother:

"You have not been consciously aware that she has been angry with you for many lifetimes. It is she that cannot forgive, for she believes that you "stole" a man from her. I see you in love with her husband, and eventually you married this man. She never forgave you for this and has wanted to punish you. Due to your own guilt, not just because of this one event but other lives also, you have allowed this individual to be your mother in several lives and to punish you, making you feel that you do not deserve.

"Now in regard to Jim and Sue, you could again repeat this old pattern. However, I feel that you also need to trust your feelings and to see that it is possible to love without pain. Interestingly, you have drawn to you a situation with another woman involved, but Sue is not your mother. I feel that you need to have perspective on this relationship with Jim. I feel that it could be long lasting, and of course, intimate, but not in the way you might think. I feel for now that you need to trust that love is not pain. You need to affirm that love brings more love. Learning to truly love both Jim and Sue can bring even more love into your life. You are, on the surface, creating the same kind of drama. Without this perspective and new growth, I sense the potential for pain and struggling, but you are different. This is a challenge you have arranged to see that you are different. Your relationships go deeper than the surface. Do not allow fear to come in. I feel that you need to see how you have changed. Love always brings more love."

Sandy chose to believe what Gay was saying about her, that she had changed and that she could have more choice in how a relationship would develop. For a while, there was some fleeting sexual involvement but eventually the relationship fell into a comfortable intellectual rapport that was satisfying to Jim and Sandy. She also maintained a comfortable ease with Sue, enjoying her company during those rare moments when they would be alone together. That situation has turned out so far to be the last of such relationships in Sandy's life. She needed to learn that she could let go of her guilt and change. She also tipped her hat to her former therapist, recognizing that indeed her mother had been influencing this pattern in much deeper ways than she would have ever thought.

The Emersons, referred to in Chapter 2 during the discussion on families, are a close knit group who care deeply about one another, so when David fell in love with his brother's wife, the entire family felt the shock waves. Sandy and Sheila heard about it first from their mother. She called for a session with Gay, naturally upset about what was happening in her family. Gay gave her reassurance and recommended that she "separate herself from her family." Shortly afterward, David had a session. The situation was intense. John was angry with David. Cher, John's wife and David's lover, was threatening suicide. David felt guilty and responsible. Gay very quickly outlined the underlying motivations of each of them, putting the situation into a perspective that illustrated how each of them contributed to the creating of this reality and how each of them might grow and learn from what was happening:

"You [David] are not admitting what it is that you want in this situation. I feel that you were not honest about what you wanted (or did not want) at the start, and this has created additional problems. I am not making judgments, simply helping you to see that it is important to be *clear* about your intentions. This has always been a problem for you and this is not the first "predicament" that you have found yourself in. Increasingly, I see you taking risks and often you seem to be pulled in many directions but in the end you have often been saved, seemingly by magic. So you take greater and greater risks in your life, personal and otherwise.

"I feel that there has always been a desire to be caught and perhaps punished for deeds no one knew of, and in this instance, you drew to you a situation that could not help but be explosive. Recognize that you created this situation. I am not certain that you want Cher to live with you, and if this is so, you need to say this to her now. Otherwise, I feel more of a struggle. Her behavior is her way of manipulating both you and John. A part of her enjoys being in the middle. Her crisis and feelings are her way of avoiding personal responsibility for what is happening. Here she can simply be emotional and not be responsible. She was a mother to you and John and that she favored John, or so you thought. Subconsciously you drew this to you so that you could truly have what John has, but I do not see that this is what you truly wanted. You wanted to receive what John had, but not to become so involved with Cher. It has as much to do with John as with Cher. Cher has not been happy for a long time but she has not wanted to accept responsibility for her unhappiness either. There is a search here for someone to take care of her, someone she can say makes her happy or unhappy.

"You must, I feel, step back and think deeply about what you want in your own life and not permit yourself to be manipulated. Your guilt is this manipulation also. You have, I feel, been—yes, I will say it—manipulated and I feel that you and John do not necessarily need to move far apart because of this. Yet that, of course, is obviously a possible outcome of this. Do not let guilt stay with you. First of all, begin to realize that you did nothing wrong, and you must tell yourself that you are not a bad person. This is important, for John is very angry and sending you the message that you are bad. Remain clear on this. Also send John love, for I feel that you have been brothers many times and, although there have been many struggles and intense rivalry, still there is potential for closeness. You have shared a lot; perhaps sharing a woman is not so strange, considering what you have shared through many lives. In a deep level, John has in his own way agreed to this event.

"I see that he also has not been happy and did not know what to do about this. This event has brought a climax to his unhappiness and doubts, and he also needed to have this happen. He has been very angry for a long time. Now he has a focus for his anger. John always likes to have reasons for feelings. I feel that, underneath, you know where you are in regard to this relationship, but you are afraid for Cher. She is quite strong. No matter what happens, recognize that you are not responsible. She also creates her destiny by not acting responsible and guilty, perhaps you will ultimately help her to see this. She is in this existence to learn that she alone is responsible for her own happiness and unhappiness. Simply believe that you have shared love with someone and that this is not a bad thing. What makes this so "bad" is each individual's perspective, not the particular situation."

Two stormy years pass. John shouted at Cher that he wished David were dead. Cher and John separated and eventually divorced. John remained angry with David. David and Cher continued to be together, both assuming that they would marry.

Sometime during these years, Cher was regressed into a past life that she shared with David and John. This life was in feudal England. John was the landowner. David and Cher lived together on a farm and loved each other very much. She reported that his presence brought her happiness. John, as landowner, insisted on his "rights" and forced Cher to have sex with him, as was the custom of the time. David was then killed by soldiers, and the implication was that John had been responsible.

Christmas, that second year, came. David bought Cher a ring and tickets to Mexico, asking her to marry him. She rejected him, breaking off the relationship completely without any apparent reason even to herself. He was devastated and became chronically depressed. Shortly after the rejection, however, he had a dream. In the dream he was working in Colorado. Cher was searching for him and came to him but treated him coldly. The dream then ended, but as it faded, David heard words that sounded "Biblical," stating that "All that was yours will be restored unto you in six months."

About April, he began to feel his anger toward Cher. It felt good, as he had been depressed for months. In June, she called him and he blasted her with an hour's worth of anger. He was surprised that she stayed on the phone. She even called him again. This time she asked to see him, to talk it all out. They made a date. He sent her a confirming note with the date of the weekend they were to meet which she misread and appeared at the meeting a week earlier, believing that David had stood her up. She was furious.

Eventually they cleared up the misunderstanding and arranged a new meeting time. They met on a Friday night. Everything went well between them until Saturday afternoon when David was struck with intense abdominal pain and cramping. They thought it was food poisoning. It went on for hours. Interestingly, this kind of attack had occurred with David six other times in the past four years, usually when he was with Cher. As the time passed this time, the pain concentrated into one sharp note in his side. He talked about going to a hospital but instead fell asleep about one o'clock Sunday morning. An hour later, he awoke to find the pain gone and himself immersed in a feeling of freedom such as he had not felt in a long, long time. He said to Cher, "We are free. The karma is over."

At the time he uttered those words, he had not thought through what they meant. Later, he and Cher realized that it was necessary for her to be with him as he went through a reenactment of the feudal lifetime. As he explained to Sandy,

"We had to resolve that death. She had to be with me while I went through the death this time and realize that I had not left her intentionally." He feels that the sharp pain in his side was a memory of having been stabbed in that past life. John's wish that he would die, Cher's misreading of his note, her distrust of him for no apparent reason, and the recurring abdominal pain all point to the need for this resolution. He also reported that his long-term depression lifted and he felt himself normal once again. He and Cher are not currently seeing each other but they are fine with that decision.

David's mother also told Sandy that the winter before these events, David and John were snowbound for several days alone in a cabin that the family owned in Wisconsin. That confinement forced them to deal with their issues and now they are close again.

Speaking about another such triangle with a young woman who came to talk to her, Gay again reiterates her clear, straightforward perspective on the entangled messes that we humans create with our confused, often guilt-ridden thinking:

"In relationships there is actually no such thing as a triangle for each relationship is separate unto itself. For you, it is important to let go of the guilt. It is not possible to take someone away from another person. You believe this is possible for it seems as though it happened to you in other lives. You have been a "victim" of this kind of a circumstance in a prior life; a man you loved left you and began living with your sister."

Gay continued talking to this woman about her "need to have revenge" for having felt herself a "victim." No one can steal away another for no one owns another. Relationship exists only in the moment that it is occurring. As we live more and more in each moment, we can let go of these complicated guilts and angers fed by our own thoughts and beliefs about the nature of reality.

Sandy was forced to face some murky reality of her own creation a few years ago as she got in touch with a habitual thought pattern that permeated her relationship with Len. As described throughout these chapters, she was learning about her part in the co-creating of their relationship. She was beginning to realize how he withdrew for her, how she emoted for him, how indeed they cooperated to keep their particularly frustrating patterns going. This time, she really caught herself in an embarrassing contribution to that pattern. Over the years, she would stage various dramas to "end" the relationship, declaring to all who would listen that it was "over," that she was through being "victimized" by his uncaring indifference, that she was going to create a viable, meaningful relationship in her life with someone who "really" loved her. This was a scenario so common, her friends would roll their eyes and moan, "There she goes again."

Then she found out how it would happen. She was always jealous of Len. Based on his previous behavior and reputation, she thought that he would "betray" her with other women. The reality of those betrayals, if they existed at all, was inconclusive and ultimately unimportant to their relationship and she knew it! That did not stop her, however, from creating fantasies in her mind in which he hurt her by being with another woman. She imagined running into him at a particular restaurant or art gallery. He was with someone strikingly beautiful and talented and she was devastated. She elaborated on this theme in exquisite detail, her emotions building to a crescendo that resulted in a nervous stomach and an irritable disposition. She then forgot what she had imagined. A few days later, she did it again. This repeated itself over several months until the internal pressure was so great that she again staged a "breakup," usually over some slight, characteristic behavior of his that, in normal circumstances, she would have easily accepted and ignored. When she caught herself in this habitual thought pattern, she was appalled. She had been doing it for years and had not been fully aware of its existence or its implications. She was telepathically "telling" him to be with other women! She was also creating unnecessary and painful emotional feelings for herself, as well as stupid dramas in their relationship.

Recognizing that this thought pattern was an old habit, she became determined to change it. She put a rubber band on her wrist and every time she caught herself in a fantasy of this kind, she stopped the thoughts and snapped the rubber band. She had a red, sore wrist for a while. At first, she caught herself toward the end of the fantasy, the negative feelings already building within her. As time went by, however, she caught herself earlier and earlier in the drama, until eventually she sensed the fantasy about to start and stopped herself. As she went through this process, she realized that she was "emptying" out a space in her mind and that, for now, she needed to replace the old, destructive and habitual thought pattern with something positive to counter its effects. She began playing a game in her mind. Each time she caught herself and snapped the rubber band, she practiced affirmations about love in her mind. It became a challenge to see how many different ways she could affirm love in her life. "I deserve love," "I deserve to love," "I deserve to be shown love, to show love," and so on.

Len remained the same, perhaps teasing her a little less about "possible" women in his life. She soon found though that the need for dramas lessened, and for a year or so afterwards, the relationship went smoothly. Eventually, other issues arose but these came out of deeper sources, not simply Sandy's overactive imagination.

Looking honestly at our interactions with others, particularly our lovers, gives us the opportunity to watch ourselves in action as we create our reality. We can learn and grow by facing our own beliefs which we accumulate from our pasts and project into our future with the patterns those thoughts and beliefs have established. It is in our present that we can discover our future. Discovering what we believe, what we think, gives us the power to change, to let go of old limiting thoughts and beliefs. We then need to discover what we want and concentrate on that. It sounds easy and it could be if we let it. Why not? Our freedom lies in accepting that we have the power to create, simply and with love.

Chapter XII

Sex: Doing It? and With Whom?

Telepathic encounters, past-life spillovers into present reality, and awareness of deep psychic bonds all lead to an enhancement of sexual activity in a relationship. Feeling the presence of a missed lover in a dream or vision sharpens desire. Playing out the roles of past-life encounters during fantasy enlivens sexual fun. And, on those rare occasions when awareness of the depth of those encounters arises during the sex act and the partners make love to many at once, the intensity of that merger can take one into sexual heights previously undreamed, unknown.

Sandy wrote the following poem during a short, but intense sexual relationship occurring ten years before this writing. The man was a yoga instructor who tried hard to believe that he could overcome his sexual desires. He and Sandy had felt an immediate attraction. During their stormy relating, Sandy, through regression and from Gay, learned of several lifetimes influencing them. She also experienced intense visions in the night while lying next to him. These were visions of other meetings far away and long ago. Gay told of two lifetimes as twins and one as mates, all occurring before recorded history in the time we think of as Atlantis.

Internal Conversations

"I love you and I'm scared."
Words on the outskirts of my mind.

Butterflies spin through my physical self,
tickling until my innard walls contract,
then swell with a surging thrust,
and, begin again . . .
Buzzing thoughts rise and fall,
darting here and there until a circle forms
around the edges of my mind,
each chasing after the others,

round and round. . .
"I'm tired of metaphysics."
Words, words, words—hammering,
demanding words—replacing feelings.
"I'm sick of words."

"Avoid attachment," you say.
"It's always Desire that brings
pain. Avoid pain. Detach."
"I can love without attachment," I boldly claim.
I think I can. I think I do. Why then am I so scared?
Because I know I can't. I know I don't.
And neither do you
love without desire,
love me without desire,
love me?

Fear. Fear of pain. Fear of no pain.
You. Me. One. Two.
The same. Mind-Body-Spirit. All are one as close as
two can be—once split from one cell, grown in one
womb—not once but twice, and mates
another time.
Long separation through time and space,
many explorations in a myriad of forms with
no touching, no merging, always seeking—
Now BE-ing together again. Intense joy, and intense fear. . .
So, words, words, words.
We understand their meaning
but go not beneath their meaning.
They become clubs to beat and shape us into desireless form. . .
to satisfy our fear.

"I love you and I'm scared."
"I worried that I was the only one. . ."

You left me recently. Your body wasn't there.
I thought you were gone.
You weren't.
Your image, rising in a dream,
boldly demanding dinner and a movie. . .
"Now that you've finished with that nonsense."

Robed figures walking through
treed, green hills intently

arguing metaphysical principles. . .
The words are now forgotten,
the reality of the scene emotionally remains.
A world long removed from conscious history
where we once lived and loved together
lost for eons to our conscious minds. . .

But now you're back, even when you're gone.
(1978)

This relationship brought into focus cultural beliefs about sex that evidently had been part of Sandy's consciousness, yet below her awareness. Her lover was a former Catholic who now espoused a philosophy mixed with Zen Buddhism and Hinduism. Even during the stormy affair, Sandy felt that he had transferred his belief in sexual sin from one form of repressive doctrine to another.

The deep seated belief that sexual expression is somehow "dirty" or "sinful" runs through the moralistic codes of many religions. The descent into the body is seen as a "fall," and subsequently, enjoyment of that body is seen as bad or "sinful." Sandy and Sheila had been working through some of these beliefs during those early years together in the late 1970s. During that time they often met men who brought their fears and guilts to the surface. Two areas of conflict emerged for them. One was that sexuality, sexual feelings and expression, conflicted with spirituality and their ability to experience spiritual reality. The other, more Sandy's than Sheila's, surrounded the conflict described elsewhere in this book between intimacy and creative expression. Sandy's learning had been to put sexual expression into perspective. Years ago, shortly after their first encounter, Gay laughingly told her that she needed to concentrate more on her creative work and less on men, that indeed she could have both instead of limiting herself to one or the other. At that time she was biased in favor of the men. Gay addressed these conflicts during a private session in 1979:

"There is no conflict between expressions of sexuality and spiritualism. Just as life is an expression of sexuality itself, you are free and you are protected. Sexual expression is meant to be a part of life. The reason that many religious people deny themselves this expression is that they are not expressing life in any way that is truly religious. Others are simply following rules that they feel will give them a reward in the future. Many do not understand the true nature of sex and its role in life. This is a part of life that you are ready to resolve even further, but I feel that you both are already living a life that shows an understanding here. Repression is not a healthy way. You realized that. Do not let others' ideas or rules affect you, even psychically."

(Sandy asked about her sexual relationship with Len which had always been the most successful part of their relating. Of course, it was because of Len that she most often curtailed her creative expression.)

"You deserve to feel good about this part of your relationship. I feel that you also judge yourself from what others' rules might be. You are also approaching this in a straight forward manner, asking for and receiving what you want. There need be no guilt. None of the activity interferes with spiritual growth. I see that you can have both and be both creative and spiritual at the same time. It is important to emphasize that sex entered into fully is a spiritual experience. I see that it has its place along side all of nature. Everything that exists exists because of sexual energy. The plants, trees, animals, the machinery, buildings, towns, cities—everything is sexual energy. Actually, the physical expression of sex can lead to greater creativity for it leaves you much more open and sensitive— physically, emotionally and psychically. You can be sensitive to your environment and the creative process can be enhanced, but it is up to you. No choice is necessary."

And so sex is an expression of life. As such it becomes an area in which we can play with our thoughts and beliefs to discover more and more about our creative abilities. Once seen in this perspective, old moralistic judgments fade away. Even the onset of AIDS, an event occurring long after Gay's words to Sandy and Sheila, can be seen as a creative reflection of cultural beliefs and judgments rather than a moralistic judgment from an angry God. We are expressing life as we believe it to be. Life does not punish us for its expression through us. It is the working through of these beliefs, then, that becomes our individual challenge as we learn more and more about our power to create our lives consciously.

Carolyn wrote to Sheila and Sandy from the Middle East where she lived with her engineer husband. She had had one session with Gay through the mail about two years before this letter. Subsequently, she had been opening spiritually to many new concepts and experiences, some of which included new sexual encounters. "I really feel that people have been 'sent' to me to help me, especially these last two years. I also feel confused by these relationships as last year it was mainly men. I have had sexual relationships with several of them. I do not feel that has been wrong but my upbringing, of course, tells me it's wrong. I asked for an answer to this all year and finally felt that I should continue until I had a strong feeling that I should not make love to other men. But then I also wonder if I just don't want to hear the answer? My brother and I agree on this, that making love to people you care for is just not a 'great sin,' and I have always held my brother in high regard. Also, could it be that it has been right for me but that this will change sometime? I'm also confused about the whole thing of spiritual growth and 'higher levels' and sexual energy being of 'lower levels.' I also know that right now I don't feel good about stopping these relationships and that I have been expecting that if I should decide to stop I would feel that stopping was what I wanted and that would 'feel good' to me. Or do I need to learn self-discipline and not listen to the lower self?"

Carolyn's stream-of-consciousness ramblings certainly reflects the struggles that we create with our confused beliefs about sexual energy. Gay addresses her personally here but also speaks to us all:

"You must trust your impulses in regard to your sexual relationships and realize that you are in the process of learning. There were many rules that were given to you as a child. I feel, though, that you only pretended allegiance to these rules to please your parents. You always saw beyond the rules, but there was fear of punishment if you broke the rules. The fear of punishment remains with you today. You must realize though that you are the only one that can punish yourself. You are deeply afraid of too much pleasure, for you feel that as far as you immerse yourself in pleasure, you must then experience the same degree of pain, and so you have not let go.

"Your recent sexual explorations are a result of asking for higher energies. The energy you seek is part of sexuality and your sexual being needs to be explored. You must trust that you will not lose control and that you are reacting to restore harmony to your psyche.

"For many years, there was a repression of sexual feelings. As a young girl you believed yourself to be without sexual feelings and yet these feelings are a part of being alive. Your father was afraid of seeing you as a sexual being and so you never expressed this part of yourself. Now it cries for expression. Let this be and rejoice that you are seeking balance. Trust that you can be as you are and that you will find the harmony that you seek. It has been important for you to know that men find you attractive. Your father had difficulties relating to women, and so you developed many feelings of insecurity around sex. Your fear of letting a man see you losing control is due to your father's influence. It is time to let go. A few years ago, you decided to let go of this influence. Your physical life's events conspire to help this process and that is what is happening. By not resisting, you naturally grow and you are letting go. You are simply changing. Do not worry whether this is permanent or temporary. Simply live each day separately. Your husband is very much like your father, and you need to feel yourself as a separate individual in order to resume closeness with him. Trust that this is possible."

Carolyn needed to allow herself her sexual explorations in order to grow. She needed, as we all do, to trust her feelings. Even in the confusion of her questioning, she seemed to know that that was important for her.

Janet was afraid of all feelings. She came to Sandy and Sheila for a number of sessions because she was having marital difficulties. She had always been a "good girl" who did what she thought others wanted of her. She never "felt" angry with anyone but tried hard to be reasonable and pleasing. Part of her complaint included a statement that she did not enjoy sex and wanted no part of it. Gay saw the sexual difficulty as part of her entire personality:

"I feel your attitude toward sex is a part of a general feeling of wanting to remain in control. Surrendering yourself sexually gives you a feeling of losing control, being out of control, and for now you need to feel in control. You see, you have chosen this reaction also. Recognize it as a choice. Allow yourself to have this choice. I feel that for too many years you have allowed others to say how you were to behave, and you are, in a sense, rebelling by not responding. That too must be seen as all right. That is your choice. See it as a choice. Become conscious."

In order to take her power in this situation, Janet needed to realize that she was choosing not to enjoy sex. Once she took responsibility for her own responses, she could then choose to change her situation, when and if she desired to do so. Greta came with the same complaint, she did not enjoy sexual relations. The influences affecting her included a past-life experience:

"You have a feeling that you are bad and that you do not deserve such sexual pleasure. I feel that here it is not so much a problem sexually but that you choose men that are not able to accept love from you. You feel this and it is inhibiting you. I see a prior life as a prostitute in Paris. This life is affecting you now. You need to let go of guilt. The men that are often interested in you were with you in this prior life. That connection has caused you to be unable to relax fully. You need to let go of this deep memory and to give yourself more. I also feel that your mother is still influencing you. Her experiences with sex when very young were painful. As you continue to work psychically at breaking the bond with her, you will find yourself much more relaxed in a sexual setting.

"You need to believe that in a sexual relationship you do not have to perform or do anything. Allow yourself to accept. Simply direct the love out from your body in a psychic sense. Do nothing on a physical level. I see you choosing men who ask you to help them sexually and on a physical plane. Do nothing. Do nothing deliberately, and be conscious of receiving. Give the love psychically. That is enough for now. It is important to practice receiving. I do not say never to do anything, for I feel you naturally will, but balance needs to be achieved. If this means doing nothing, it will prove most beneficial. Trust that you can draw to you a man that will understand you."

A past life as a Parisian prostitute and a mother giving her messages that sex is painful meant to Greta that she could not receive sexual pleasure. For women, however, it is often their fathers that determine their ability to experience sexual satisfaction.

Both Carmen and Betty were beautiful women. They knew many men and seldom had difficulty attracting lovers. Both, however, did have difficulty enjoying those lovers and felt frustrated most of the time. Gay talked to Carmen about her mother's influence, then about her father:

"Many of your mother's beliefs about men were given to you, and at deeper levels (most probably unconscious), she does not want you to be any more satisfied than she was, and yet consciously she says she wants to see you happy. This has created conflict within, for you are not sure that you believe what she says. I also feel that you do not want to let anyone take your father's place.

There is a strong bond between you and your father, for you have been lovers before. I feel that he does not want anyone to replace him with you. Of course, this too runs far beneath the surface; yet, nonetheless, it has a very definite impact and influence. You do need to reassure your father psychically of your love. He is not sure that you love him. Respect, in his mind, is equated with love, and so he tries to keep a hold on you psychically simply because he is not sure of your love.

"In other existences where you were lovers, there were often situations when he felt jealous. In one lifetime, you had many lovers and he wanted to marry you. You chose another. In another existence, he loved you from a distance. You were quite unattainable. The situation could be eased if, as part of your affirmations, you could affirm your love for him. This may appear to you to be like further increasing the tie you wish to be freed from. However, it will actually give you the freedom you need. You have not always wanted this freedom. At the same time, you do this exercise, realize there is ambivalence and you enjoy this bond also. What you need to realize is that you deserve a relationship without so much struggle. Perhaps "snuggling instead of struggling."

Carmen had come in complaining about her father's irrational demands on her as a daughter. She also complained of struggles with her lovers. She had not perceived a connection between the two issues. Interestingly, her own ambivalence and need for clarity in the situation contributed to her discomfort. With Betty the past lives with her father were even more blatantly influential:

"Your soul has explored many lifetimes, and I see many lives where your father was your lover. There is a very close connection here. I feel that the other lives are influencing you now, for your father remains quite possessive of you. This, of course, is at a psychic level. You may or may not already be aware of this but there is a great desire to please him. This affects the relationships you have with other men. Many to whom you are drawn are quite similar to your father, and it is important for you not to try so hard to please them. Concentrate more on your own desires and your own life. I feel a disappointment in your life that you have not been able to recapture the past relationships with your father. This has been very frustrating. You search for the perfect man, and you are missing ones that could love you very deeply."

Sally came in to Sandy's office for a counseling session. She thought that perhaps a past-life regression would help her with the difficulties she was having with relationships. In the previous five years, two devastating affairs had left her feeling confused and worthless. These men, she related to Sandy, were much like her father; they both withheld their feelings from her and subtly put her down in ways that undermined her self-confidence. She said that she had been close to her father as a young child, but when she reached adolescence, he cut her off emotionally, even to the point of becoming hostile toward her. She felt that he was much more hostile toward her than her sister. With her brothers, he was also fine. She did not understand this, but she felt that it was responsible for her lack of confidence. She also complained of sexual difficulties, claiming to achieve orgasm only through masturbation. This too was a source of frustration that she wanted to change.

Sandy put her in trance intending to lead her into a past life which might explain some of these problems. As soon as she got to the point where impressions could flow, she blocked. Sandy tried many different approaches, but Sally could not relax enough to allow the process to work. As Sandy worked with her, she began to get a strong feeling that Sally's father was in the way of her progress. She decided to confront this directly and began a chakra cutting process (See Chapter 15) between Sally and her father in which the past life information surfaced. There were two chakra points which dramatically illustrated what was going on between them. At the sexual chakra, Sally sensed that they had been lovers. As they continued up through the seven chakras, nothing came up except some confusion at the solar plexus and the heart, but when they reached the third eye chakra (the telepathic or psychic center), Sally saw clear images of them making love.

After Sandy brought her out of trance, they talked about what had happened. Sally confessed that she had had fantasies about making love with her father but never dreamed that it actually might have happened. She admitted that she had always felt that he was "the only lover for her." Sandy stressed the need for her to realize that his withdrawing from her was because of his own confused feelings as she became a woman. Sally had interpreted this as "against" her and drew conclusions about her own desirability that were negatively influencing her ability to have successful sexual relationships. Sandy stressed over and over that it was very important for her to let him go on psychic levels so that she could begin living a freer, fuller sexual life.

This man chose to withdraw from his daughter rather than risk acting out his sexual feelings for her. He most likely did not realize the psychological damage that he was inflicting upon her. How often does lack of awareness of such past-life experience result in even worse damage when it is acted upon by the parent? How many cases of damaging incest occur because people do not understand where their feelings may be coming from? How much guilt do people suffer because they have "unclean" thoughts toward their children?

Sandy was fortunate because she had access to the past-life influences operating between her and her oldest son. She often found herself attracted to him and sometimes felt his attraction to her. His jealousies, as described in an earlier chapter, made sense when cast into this larger perspective. When he entered adolescence and began dating, Sandy found herself extremely critical of the girls that he brought home. None of them were good enough. She found herself feeling that she wanted him all to herself. That is not an uncommon feeling between parents and their children, but it is one that often leads to confusion and guilt and then to subsequent misunderstandings and unnecessary fighting. Sandy was able to discuss her feelings with Sheila and sometimes even with Steven, putting them in a proper perspective that included past-life influences. Because of that, these incidences became family jokes rather than family disasters.

We have been talking throughout this book about psychic influences on relationships. This next story reminds us that the influences upon us are not always psychic but can include elements that are more psychological than we might want to admit. A young woman called Sandy on behalf of her good friend, Jennifer. Jennifer had been experiencing "spirit activity" in her apartment, and they were quite concerned about it and wanted to know what to do. There were books moved, record albums off the shelves, pictures rearranged on the walls, and finally an occurrence that precipitated the call to Sandy. Returning home late and tired after working a night shift at the suburban hospital where she is a nurse, Jennifer fell asleep with her uniform still on. She woke up later with all her clothes off. She went into the bathroom and found the sink full of dirt.

She knew it had been clean earlier. Scared, she left and went to the home of one of her friends to spend the remainder of the night. In the morning, upon returning to her apartment, she found two wine glasses, wine, and cheese on a tray by her bed. She had not had wine or cheese in her house.

Talking to Jennifer's friend, Sandy learned that Jennifer always had been psychic. As a child, she had frequently experienced unexplainable phenomenon and once even had had a large breakfront begin vibrating as she walked by. The breakfront was so large and heavy that it took her father and two men to move it back.

Sandy agreed to talk to Jennifer and suggested that she call herself. She did the following day, excited because "the mystery was solved." When she arrived home from work at about twelve-thirty that morning, there was a man on her doorstep. She did not see him immediately but heard his steps. She turned toward him and he asked her if he could help her. She insisted that he had no business there. He said that he was simply visiting someone. She again insisted that no one there knew him and he did not belong there. He moved toward her and brushed his hand across her cheek, saying "I love you, Jennifer." He walked away. No one else ever saw him. Jennifer checked with the mailman, thinking that he would know everyone in the neighborhood, but he had never seen anyone of that description. She seemed happy though with her discovery of him and felt willing to let the entire incident drop. She was sure that he had been the intruder in her apartment and that if she simply changed the locks, everything would be fine. Sandy was not so sure that it was so simple. She decided to ask Gay about this incident, curious because of its sexual overtones and psychic nature. She asked whether or not the man was in physical reality? If so, what are the past-life connections? And what kind of influences brought about the entire incident?

"First of all, here you are not dealing with a ghost as you would think of one. The man she saw was quite "real," physically present. The ghost we are dealing with here is another "personality" present within the woman, an individual who seems quite grounded and "normal." She does, however, have an aspect of herself, call it another personality if you wish, that acts out the sexual repressions that are part of this main personality. It is not a personality that is in any way harmful to this individual. It is the part of her that enjoys being sexual and is, indeed, quite free in her sexual behavior. There is no remembrance because of some deep-seated guilts here. It is this other self that gave the key to her apartment to the man she saw. She met him at a bar not far from her home. And, she has been having sex with him. Often this "other" part of herself awakens at night when she has fallen asleep and sometimes even leaves the apartment. It is quite true that she does not remember any of these activities. There is too much danger to the personality who is "good" to remember the one who likes to indulge in what might be termed "bad" behavior by the main personality. This is not a case with many personalities, just this one. It is not, at this point, dangerous in any physical sense.

"Now, there are indeed other phenomena throughout this entity's life, none more significant than the ones that you yourselves have encountered. We have here a very psychic individual who draws to her mischievous spirits. They represent the part of her that would like to be mischievous herself. The phenomena will most likely end when she accepts all parts of herself. It is doubtful, though, that this can be accomplished without some therapy and facing some deep pain. It is not time to tell her that this other "personality" exists without some preparation. In this case, some therapy would be advised before any conversation with me or any other psychic, although we must always remember that ultimately what happens is always right.

"The man involved here has, of course, past-life connections to this woman. They have been lovers many times and he is indeed falling in love with her. It may enable her to face the truth here, and I feel that he could be a support in this way to her, if she does not run away from all of this. What can you do? Actually nothing, at this point, but to send this woman energy and love. And be aware that there are many explanations to phenomena, sometimes indeed there are beings who return to continue love affairs, but in this case we have two personalities, each unaware of the other."

Sandy never heard from Jennifer again. Evidently Gay correctly sensed that she was not yet ready to face her "deep pain." At this time in her life, it apparently was easier for this woman to accept some "ghost" activity or a strange intruder, rather than face her own sexual needs.

Phil entered Sheila's office tentatively. He had had several sessions with Gay over the years, and this particular day he had taken his wife's appointment because she was out of town on business. That was fine with Sheila. She had always liked Phil and was happy to see him. As he began reviewing his questions for Gay, he hemmed and hawed, shuffling his feet and looking away from Sheila. This was unusual behavior for him and she wondered what was up. The situation became more and more tense until Sheila began feeling his intense embarrassment. She offered him a drink of water and got up to walk around herself to relieve the tension. Finally he blurted out, "I have a problem with sex. I'm obsessed with sex."

Sheila wondered what possibly could be so terrible. Almost everyone is "obsessed with sex" at some time in their lives, she thought. Phil then confessed that he liked to dress in women's clothes, particularly underwear. Sheila had to stop herself from laughing because she had been expecting something really terrible like child molestation or rape. So he liked to dress in women's clothing? She couldn't see the problem. Any reader of newspaper advice columns knows that this is one of the most common sexual "aberrations," and certainly one of the least harmful in our culture. She tried to put him at ease by talking about the unfairness of our culture in the raising of children. Little girls are allowed to dress in masculine clothing all through their lives and no one ever notices. Little boys, on the other hand, are tightly restricted from birth to wear only "masculine" clothing. She argued that this was very unfair and that his desires were not "bad." He replied that he had gone over these arguments himself many times but had been unable to lessen his feelings of shame and disgust. Neither had he been able to stop. He worried that it was affecting his relationship with his wife. She was giving him a hard time about his cross-dressing and lately he had been turned-off sexually to her and blamed her relatively recent weight gain. They had been married for many years and had four young children. He wanted his marriage to work.

Sheila went into trance. Gay reassured him that what he was doing was not as bad as he felt it was. She then told him of a lifetime he had lived in Ireland. His mother then is his mother in this present life. She had three children in that Irish life, two girls and a boy. She doted on the boy, her last and favored child. While he was very young, she dressed him in her clothing. She did stop this behavior early so he had very little conscious memory of it. She remained attached to him, however, influencing his life with her desires. She wanted him to be a priest. He did as she wished. At the time, there was much sexual repression through Irish culture and he, in particular, was extremely repressed sexually. As a priest, he became moralistic and judgmental. He did have one sexual encounter in that lifetime with the woman who is now his present wife. He turned away from her in shame and refused to have anything to do with her subsequently. Ironically, during his late years as a priest, a man came to him to confess a liking for dressing in women's clothes. He was outraged by this confession and refused to forgive the man for his sin. He judged the man as a "horrible, execrable sinner." The man died alone and miserable.

Phil judges himself now. He has karmically set up his learning in this lifetime to atone for his harshness in a previous lifetime. It is time for him to confront the judge within himself and learn to forgive. Sheila hoped that he would be able to accomplish this within his present life.

Not everyone who cross-dresses suffers Phil's extreme anguish. It is possible, however, that past-life influences play as large a part in a person's particular fetish as do cultural, parental, and psychological influences. Curiosity is another possibility that should not be ruled out. We are creative beings, and to want to try to understand how a person of another sex might feel by cross-dressing or some other unusual behavior, could be viewed as a creative act.

Sexual preferences too can be influenced by past-life experience. Sandy and Sheila have had the opportunity of working with many homosexual people during their years of counseling. They live near New Hope, Pennsylvania, a town of highly creative people and a large gay population, and many gay people are attracted to spiritual and psychic pursuits. The two women often found homosexual people open and willing to explore the depths of their feelings, perhaps in order to understand their sexual preferences in this lifetime, which certainly can be more difficult to live with in our culture than heterosexuality.

Two men from New York City came to talk to Gay. They had been lovers for many years and were concerned about unresolved feelings. George constantly worries about Henry, afraid that something terrible might happen to him.

"You have been together in other incarnations. I see you married once and, Henry, you committed suicide for which George blamed himself. Although this had nothing to do with your relationship, it has created many feelings. The suicide was because of your work, Henry, and a feeling of being rejected. This lifetime occurred in England at the beginning of this century. There were books you had written that no one would publish because you were a woman. There was much despair and the suicide was because of this."

George and Henry were back together but this time Henry chose to be a man, perhaps because of this prior experience.

A man from Philadelphia came to Mind Matters for a past-life regression. Carl was distressed because of an intense, emotional relationship with a male lover. He had been taken with this man at first sight and subsequently had engaged in a long, dramatic affair with him, constantly trying to extricate himself emotionally but always falling back into extreme feelings. He wanted to understand what was happening to him. Most of his life was orderly and peaceful. His work went well, his previous sexual relationships ran rather smoothly, and he had an easy and comfortable relationship with his family.

Sandy guided him through a tunnel into another time and place. He found himself by a river, a woman clothed in a long heavy dress. He/she felt sad and perplexed. A man approached and he/she knew that this man was her husband. He was furious, yelling at her. He/she did not understand his anger and felt helpless. He came up, grabbing her shoulders, shaking her until he pushed her into the river. He/she struggled but the heavy skirts and petticoats soon pulled her/him under the water. After death, he/she was still confused about her husband's anger. This confusion is carried into this lifetime, where he is still trying to understand the anger. He realized that if they were both men this time, he might be able to communicate with this lover and learn what he needed to know. He now concluded that he may have to let go of this idea and go on with his life.

Our wonderful human ingenuity in creating variety in sexual expression is illustrated by Carla's life situation. She was thirty years old, married ten or so years, with three children, when she found herself attracted to women. When she could no longer deny this part of herself, she told her husband. He then confessed that he had been homosexual all of his life but also had wanted a family. They agreed to remain married, be partners in child-rearing, but each have their own lovers, hers would be female, his, male. At the time Carla came for her first session with Gay, this arrangement was working relatively smoothly. The children were now teenagers and had no inkling of their parents' sexual lives. There had been some jealousy in the early years of the arrangement but that had lessened. At the end of Carla's reading, Gay commented on their relationship:

"I will comment on you and Jay. You have been married before, several lives; however, you have not always been happy together. You lived in the Midwest at the beginning of this century in a very traditional life, a very traditional marriage, and you were both dissatisfied but did not speak of it to each other. You had no sexual interest in each other and you never thought to look elsewhere. Your sexual energy was buried deeply. For you, Carla, as a woman your energy went into civic-minded projects and your husband's into local politics. Although you respected each other, you hated the existence together. I feel you needed to be together now to allow yourselves to grow within the relationship because there is a great deal of love here and you are friends who need each other. In other lives I also see you married, never very happy, but I feel the resolution is in your present situation."

Gay's optimistic assessment for resolution was based on what was happening at the time. Sandy spoke with Carla about five years later, and the entire scene had shifted. As the children grew up, Jay's old jealousies reappeared. Carla met a woman whom she truly loved and with whom she wanted to live. Jay's relationships were not so successful and his jealousy flared. He fought her decision to leave and attempted to turn their children against her. New lessons had arisen and Carla is now learning about her power and the power of love as she rebuilds her relationships with her grown children.

A young woman struggling to deal with her sexual identity came to speak to Gay, asking about what she called her "bisexuality." Gay's answer sums up for us the possibility that we all have for creative sexual expression:

"I do wish to comment on what you call bisexuality. I feel that there is no "bisexuality." All that exists is sexuality of human beings. You need to simply allow your physical being to express itself sexually. The problems and prejudices created in your society come from denying individuals freedom to express sexuality and then dealing with the underlying rage, sometimes Violently; however, I do feel that you need to focus on yourself as a physical being and concentrate on the beauty of your physical self. It in no way negates your spirituality, for the physical and spiritual are one. Body, mind, and soul are one. You have chosen in your lives to separate these three. Many lives were intensely mental or spiritual, and now in your present life, you have had intensely physical experiences, not realizing that each of these three avenues can be a way to God, particularly if you can trust and see that all experiences are good experiences, learning experiences. I feel you do not have the problem that you think you have. It is simply a matter of trusting your total self to find balance."

Chapter XIII

Friends, Enemies and Others

Sandy's son, Griffin, was eight years old. He had a best friend, Mike. In fact, they had been best friends all their lives. Sandy and Mike's mother became friends during their pregnancies and joked that Grif and Mike started playing together while sitting side-by-side during political meetings while their big-stomached mothers fought for local justice. Griffin asked Gay about his friend Michael and why they were such good friends:

"I see a strong psychic bond here, for you were brothers before this life. You, Griffin, were a stockbroker and Mike was your brother. You helped him much in that life. I also see you as friends in Alaska. You have been close together before and so it is natural for you to be friends now."

A woman named Janice came for a session with Gay. She had the usual questions about relationships, career, and life's direction. As Sheila concentrated to go into trance, she kept picking up on the name Ann, or Anna. She asked Janice about her impression. She immediately thought of a former roommate with whom she had had a terrible fight. She had decided to put it all behind her and had not even thought about asking a question concerning the matter. Gay felt otherwise:

"This person, Anna, would like to have more control in your life now. I feel that she is not happy right now; however, it is important for you to recognize that it is time to let go of this connection fully and to live your own life. The awareness now will begin to help you to let go. Simply be aware that she thinks of you and holds some anger toward you. You simply need to know this and affirm that you are free and very strong and powerful yourself and mentally surround yourself with light. That is enough."

The thoughts of others, past-life connections, and resulting psychic bonds are influences that operate throughout all of the relationships in our lives. In this chapter, some of the more colorful variations of those influences and how they affect us will be covered. Parallel lives, probable selves, teachers from the past impinging on the present are examples of the richness of our creativity as we call on our experience to create more fully in our present.

Back in 1979, Sandy and Sheila had a joint chart done by astrologer, Jacob Schwartz. Jacob is a well-known and respected Philadelphia practitioner who developed a unique approach to astrology using a computer. In their session with Jacob, the two women learned that the astrological influences in their charts pointed to a successful and long-lasting professional relationship. Sandy's Sun sign is Aries. Sheila's is Libra. They are diametrically opposed on the Zodiac circle. The personality characteristics that each brings to the relationship compliment rather than conflict.

Over the years, Jacob's predictions have proven correct. Mind Matters runs quite smoothly with little or no friction between them. In addition, each respects the other's freedom, giving one another the space to live their personal lives in a way that promotes self-expression and growth. Sometimes, however, the closeness that they experience together brings what we might call "overlapping." This was demonstrated earlier in the book when Sandy chose to feel Sheila's feelings during the hypnosis session dealing with Sheila and Jaime's early struggles together as mother and child. Years before, Sheila had performed a similar "service" for Sandy.

During the Spring of 1979, Sandy was immersed in a period of learning that was drawing a lot of anger toward her. Two women in particular were angry at her for completely different reasons. This anger created additional turmoil during a time that Sandy already was tumbling through the chaos of her younger sister's unexpected death as well as the resumption of her relationship with Len after a year's separation. She was feeling emotionally battered from every direction.

One of the women who was angry with Sandy attended Sheila's on-going ESP class. She marched into class one Wednesday night and read a "manifesto" about how Sheila had betrayed her confidence and, therefore, did not deserve to be running such a class or counseling others. Sheila was quite stunned as she knew that Jan's anger had nothing to do with her but should have been directed at Sandy. A day or two later a similar incident occurred with the second woman, an older woman who felt that she knew what was best for Sandy and was angry that Sandy did not follow her wishes. Rather than deal directly with Sandy, she attacked Sheila, telling her that she "had much psychological work to do." Sandy, surprised by these incidents, asked Gay if indeed Sheila was "protecting" her by "taking on other people's anger" toward her?

"These are very good insights into personality. You both need to experience others' anger and separate yourself from their feelings. As you become stronger and more powerful in a real way, this may cause others to feel feelings that they have buried. Nothing will happen to you that you cannot deal with. You are protected and receive support and help from me and each other and friends. Sheila, you are seeing that you are strong enough to experience others' anger and continue on your own way. This has been possible because you have allowed others to love and take care of you when needed. In your love and concern for Sandy, you have felt that you must protect her by experiencing more than is necessary. You can end this. I feel that this session will help for now you are conscious of this; and you, Sandy, will see your real strength and your own abilities and creativity."

Sheila had handled both situations with strength. During Jan's attack in the class, she had listened carefully and then directed Jan toward thinking about her own feelings and what she, Jan, was going through, rather than feeling defensive or hurt herself. She then saw that the other class members supported her completely and joined her efforts to help Jan see the situation more clearly. In the second situation, she simply psychically separated from the woman and knew that the accusation "that she had psychological work to do" (don't we always?) was a projection of anger and refused to take it seriously. These were important steps for Sheila at that time as she had been learning to psychically "separate" herself from others, an important and necessary process in the development of her own work. Eventually, as Sandy moved through her grieving period and grew stronger, she was able to confront both women directly and deal with her own issues.

The complexity of Sandy and Sheila's relationship takes on another dimension when the influence of their "parallel" lives is considered. The concept of "parallel lives" or "counterparts," came to their attention early in their relationship. In *Being Alive Is Being Psychic,* Sandy describes her encounter with an "other self" who lived in Puerto Rico and wrote poetry, often moving in and out of mental hospitals. She had first "met" this other self during a meditation in which she experienced herself out-of-body and in his presence. Gay had then described him as an "other self." Later, the two women heard this same idea expressed by Dick Sutphen as he described "parallel lives", explorations made by our souls during the same time period in which we are currently living. Jane Roberts' Seth, in *Unknown Realities, Volume I,* discusses the same phenomenon, calling them "counterparts." These influences are really no more powerful than past-life influences or even future-life influences, inasmuch as time is illusory and everything happens in an all-encompassing *Now.*

Metaphysically, all lifetimes are occurring "at once" and that theory is crucial in that our power can then always be in our present. Another lifetime may be influencing us but because that lifetime is actually occurring "now," we can "go there," and communicate with our other aspects, thereby, making a qualitative difference in our present life. Because of our focus in the current time-space coordinate, however, the interactions on the psychic plane between ourselves and our "parallel" or "other" selves can be extremely interesting.

David Palladin visited Sandy and Sheila in the spring of 1978 to do a seminar for Mind Matters. David was an artist from Arizona who channeled several different entities, one of whom was Wassily Kandinsky, the Russian artist. David's story is written in a number of books and articles, Dick Sutphen's in particular. David was an "unconscious" medium and had given permission to his entities to speak whenever they chose. He would then lose his David-consciousness and tune out of what was happening around him, later asking to be filled in on what had occurred and what was said.

After the seminar he conducted for Mind Matters, David and his wife, Linda, went with Sandy and Sheila to dinner in New Hope, Pennsylvania. Everyone was "high" from the energy of the seminar and the table was filled with "spooks" (David's word for his entities), popping in and out with ease, voicing different opinions and offering tidbits of information. Sheila allowed Gay to talk as well and a good time was had by all, including the guests at the other tables who were more than a little perplexed at all the strange voices speaking at a table for four. During this colorful exchange of spirits and humans, Kandinsky offered Sandy and Sheila some interesting information about themselves. "You each have a parallel-self living in Portland, Oregon. The one who is Sheila's self looks like Sandy and the one who is Sandy's parallel self looks like Sheila. These two women influence you greatly."

Sheila and Sandy took this information as part of the fun of the evening; however, Gay later confirmed that this was so:

"They are there as Kandinsky said. Best not to know who they are as yet. Just be yourselves. This aids them. Use white light so they don't interfere with you. Sheila had the skin rash at the same time as her counterpart. They are stuck right now, limited in perspective. They are you two if you had not chosen to continue your work despite fear and many stumbling blocks."

At the time, this made little sense to Sheila and Sandy. Sheila had indeed just gotten over a mysterious skin rash which had no logical or medical explanation. They went on with their lives, for the moment forgetting these far-away "other selves."

Over the years, however, the two women were to be reminded periodically of their Portland counterparts. Early in 1979, Sandy once again encountered her Puerto Rican counterpart in a meditation and asked Gay what he wanted. She replied that he was back in the hospital and was asking for her help. Then she went on to say:

"Also influencing you now is the woman from Portland. Her friend (Sheila's other self) gave up working in the psychic areas and she feels very badly now. This also accounts for some of your fears. She moved from Portland to San Francisco with her husband. (the one who is Sheila?) Yes. (My counterpart is still in Portland?) Yes. Her husband came between you and this work. He is against the occult."

This session had come at a time when Sandy was feeling doubts about her work with Sheila. She felt unimportant and much like a "secretary" to Sheila's important "channeling." It was the beginning of Gay's prediction that she would eventually be doing counseling of her own. She, of course, did not know that at the time. The influence of her other selves coincided with her own self-doubt. This continued to be the pattern of the interactions over the years. There were times when she or Sheila felt depressed or sick and upset and Gay would give them further information about the circumstances of their counterparts' lives. This, of course, did not happen every time they were going through some emotional period, but at those times when Gay would refer to the counterparts, the information made sense and would often free them from the particular predicament of the time.

At one point, Sheila had been physically dizzy and disoriented for several days. She kept complaining to Sandy that she felt "drugged." They asked Gay what was going on and again she referred to the women from Portland, telling them that Sheila's counterpart was so distressed by her psychic experiences and the judgment of her family, that her husband had put her in a mental hospital where she was given heavy doses of drugs to "cure" her of her "craziness." As soon as Sheila realized the source of her discomfort, she was able to let go of the symptoms. Both women were learning how important Gay's first warning was to "use white light so that they won't interfere with you." They would send their other selves love but then wisely protect themselves.

A few years later, Sandy asked about feeling sick. At the time, Sheila had been feeling great fear about losing friends, particularly Sandy. She was afraid that Sandy or another close friend would die. Gay told them that both of Sandy's counterparts had died within the week. The Puerto Rican "self" had killed himself in despair over a woman. That was not a surprise as he had often threatened suicide during depressions that would spill over into Sandy's reality. The Portland "self," however, died in a plane crash which killed 150 people. As Sheila spoke for Gay, giving the information, she began to sob and broke the trance. She realized that she had been picking up on the death of Sandy's Portland "self" and that had intensified her feelings of impending doom. This occurred in July, 1982.

In November, 1983, Sheila experienced tremendous fear of driving on major Interstate highways. She was also experiencing painful kidney and bladder infections. They asked Gay:

"These other selves of yours both have died now. This one recent death, her name was Patricia, was killed in a freeway accident by a truck. There is some freedom here, but the transition she is making is affecting the physical body here. She died abruptly with shock to the internal organs which were crushed. Sheila's body absorbed her pain and, hence, the infections. (Why did they both die violently?) There was, as you know, a choice and for that choice we must look at the personalities.

"Your other self's name was Paulette. She and Patricia were both drama majors at one time and loved drama. They both were drawn to tragic drama and I feel that Paulette wanted to die in a tragic way because she wanted to leave a difficult relationship and did not know how. She did not want to commit suicide or do it consciously and neither did she like to prolong the decision such as being ill for a while, so this was quick and tragic. Now Patricia wanted to die like her friend did and her death was part of dying in a similar way. I feel that their deaths indeed have signified the changes and growth that the two of you have done in the past year. It has been difficult, not without struggle, but you are finding who you are and yet continuing to trust in this friendship. These two,

Paulette and Patricia, were unhealthily (I do not wish to imply a judgment, of course) but unhealthily dependent on each other, as you see with Patricia's death. You both are learning to trust in the healthiest way you can. Now we will simply send them light and they are both open to it. Let them be on their way. In this way, you will be freer."

That event in 1983, ended the incidents of influence that moved back and forth between these counterparts. Sandy's frequent depressions lessened and those that did occur had causes that she could easily pin-point in her present life. Sheila struggled less with judgments of her work and suffered fewer unexplainable physical symptoms.

As stated earlier, Sheila and Sandy's professional life has gone relatively smoothly over the years. There was one period of time, however, that was particularly intense and seemed to threaten their work. About one month before Sandy's book, *Being Alive Is Being Psychic,* was to be released, Sheila dropped by her house and announced that she no longer wanted to do the sessions with Gay. She wanted to quit. At this point, they had been working together, doing the private sessions with Gay and joint workshops for about six years.

Sandy was astounded by this announcement but in keeping with their vow to respect each other's decisions, she said nothing. Later, however, she wrote in her journal: "Sheila came by yesterday afternoon to talk. She doesn't want to do readings anymore. She was afraid that I'd be angry. I wasn't, of course, but I find myself very anxious today. I knew the time would come when we couldn't continue to work as we have and also that I would eventually want to be freed of the secretarial role that I've been playing for years [Sandy was still taking Gay's words down in shorthand and typing transcripts of all the sessions], but there's a lot of change occurring right now and I'm anxious. I've put all my energy into the work with her and Gay and I've passed up other opportunities. It scares me to think that it might come to nothing. She has to do what she needs to do, of course, but I'm having feelings of being abandoned before I'm ready. I know they're just feelings and not reality as I'm really ready for a change but not knowing how it's going to evolve is a little overwhelming, especially with the damn book and all the time I've invested in it. I need to work on my feelings about it but don't know if I want to go to her. I don't want her to feel guilty but then that's her problem."

As usual, Sandy's journal writing reflected all of her inner conflicts. She wanted to respect Sheila's decision. She was also feeling abandoned, particularly since the book was about to come out and the book was about Sheila and Gay and would bring new business to Mind Matters. She knew that she needed to work with her feelings but did not want to upset Sheila.

The next few days were terrible. Sandy was depressed and kept having upsetting dreams which reflected her confusion about Sheila and Mind Matters. Finally in one dream, Sheila and Alan came to her to tell her how "wonderful" their lives were now that they had "settled down." She woke up furious, yelling at her cat, then bursting into tears. She called Sheila.

It turned out that Sheila too had been going through powerful feelings about the situation. They talked and cried together and both realized that they were facing some deep fears that had come to the surface because of the upcoming book publication. Sheila was afraid that her freedom would be lost, that the book's potential success would mean that she would have to do hundreds and hundreds of readings, speak to large groups, appear on television and radio, all of which meant to her that she would never have any time for herself. Sandy was afraid of both success and failure and being left alone with either.

This talk relieved the tension but it wasn't until after the party celebrating the book's release that Gay finally put the issues into perspective. Again, a quote from Sandy's journal describes her feelings and explains what Gay was to say: "Sheila came over for me to talk to Gay but as we began I felt angry and said that I didn't want a lot of general reassurance and crap! I wanted specific help. That declaration led to a dialogue between us and I realized that I was angry with Sheila because I felt that she was denying her responsibility for the book and our work together. I yelled at her, 'You're a part of this and, damn it, you can't run away from it.' I was furious and hadn't known it before."

Gay explained the situation with past-life information:

"This area of feelings was the best possible energizer. It is important to allow it and to see it as growth. You are still angry at being abandoned, Sandy, abandoned in your present life many times. You and Sheila were married, not married, no, lovers. A child was born, illegitimate, and you were left alone, Sandy, with this child. In this existence, Len was your father and you could not tell him of this child and so you were totally alone. This is influencing you now as well as old abandonments in your present life. From the moment of awareness in the womb you felt abandoned by your mother, and the book is like a birth now and even your mother's lack of acknowledgment is symbolic of another abandonment, and you have also drawn Len's noninvolvement. It is very important for you to have this happen for perhaps a final letting go of the feelings of abandonment. They are coming at you from many directions, you see, all hitting at the time of a "birth." Now you both have tremendous energy that has been sent out, and Sheila must simply see herself as already free. None of this has anything to do with freedom. You are both strong and I feel that each of you can contribute energy in terms of dealing with your feelings as you are, and simply see yourselves as free. The consciousness is indeed what creates your reality.

"The book is a physical step in a direction you have needed to go. The book has an energy, a consciousness of its own, a beauty of its own. You were, with the book, shall we say, a mother, and in a sense, we could say that Sheila is the father energy here and you created this entity. Now where it takes you is still your own decision. Simply let yourselves become clear separately and meditate on light going out surrounding the book."

In subsequent years, Sandy and Sheila were to experience many changes in their work. Shortly after the book's "birth," Sheila did become busier and Sandy could no longer transcribe all the sessions. Sheila began working alone and recording the sessions on tape. Later they realized that this was an important step for Sheila, because now she could recognize the strength and power that she had gained over the years. Sheila also found that she determined when and where she appeared publicly, and in keeping with who she is, she has chosen to maintain a low profile, quietly teaching classes and holding her private sessions. Sandy very soon became involved in her own private practice, counseling people using the metaphysical education that she had gained while typing Gay's words over the years. Both women began doing workshops and seminars separately, as it became economically feasible to spread their time and energy in different directions. Now Mind Matters continues, each woman referring people to the other as the need arises, their work different yet complementary.

We humans occasionally engage in relationships with people who, at some time or another, become our "enemies," people who struggle with us for some reason or another. Sandy became involved with the woman called Jan mentioned earlier in such a struggle and, for a short period of time, Jan became an "enemy," negatively influencing Sandy. Gay commented on this influence:

"There are influences you are sensitive to. (Such as?) Such as the negative attacks that you have had since you began seeing Len again. These attacks are because of your own guilt, and you have chosen someone to do this who is very angry anyway. (Jan?) Yes."

And so Jan's anger had more cause than simply Sandy's behavior, and Sandy needed to look at her own feelings in order to protect herself from that anger. "Negative" or "psychic" attacks are real enough in that the thoughts and feelings of others can influence us, affecting how we feel and behave. It is important, however, to realize that every event that we experience is "co-created." It is important to be aware of the negative thoughts and feelings of others directed at us. We do not have to allow those thoughts and feelings to affect us. When we are vulnerable because of our own need to learn, then the effect of such "attacks" is powerful.

Sheila became the object of a well-planned "attack" by an angered wife who feared losing her husband. She had been doing a series of sessions for Dan, a man extremely successful in the business world but unhappy in his marriage. He was trying to sort out his own feelings, attempting to make a decision about whether to stay in a marriage that he felt limited his creativity. He wanted the marriage and felt that the information he was receiving from Gay was helping him understand the issues he and his wife needed to confront. His wife, however, wanted things to stay as they had always been, her husband at home and "good," never looking at the issues in front of them. She was terrified of change. He, on the other hand, needed the challenge of change and growth. Her solution to this problem was to attack Sheila as the cause of all her difficulties.

Sheila received her new client into the office, asking in her usual way if there was a particular issue that the client would like Gay to address.

The woman before her seemed strained and nervous but that was not unusual for a first session. She outlined a terrible concern for her daughter who, she claimed, was only thirteen years old and already seriously involved with drugs. Sheila was sympathetic. She listened carefully then went into trance. Gay addressed the issue at great length with many details from past-life situations. When Sheila finally came out of trance, the woman was defiantly staring at her, an ugly, smug look on her face. "I knew it!" she screamed. "You are a fraud. You have been hoodwinking my husband and all the many people who come to you. I've caught you and I'm going to let the world know who you really are!"

Sheila was astounded. She was not even completely out of trance and the words coming at her made no sense. She shook her head. "What are you talking about?" she asked.

The woman then revealed that she was Dan's wife. She had never accepted the information given to him about the dynamics of her marriage, feeling that if he simply remained at home with her, all would be fine. She was now going to prove to him that she was right and everything that Gay had said to him was a lie! The daughter was fictional, made up to prove that Sheila was a fraud. She marched out of the office, her head held high.

Sheila was devastated. How could Gay betray her like that? Why wouldn't she have known that the woman was lying? Where did all the material in the reading come from if the situation was not real? She plunged into the worst self-doubt that she had ever experienced, questioning every session that she had ever done. She went to Sandy and Alan for comfort. Neither of them experienced the same doubts that were flooding her. "There's an explanation," Sandy insisted. "We simply need to look at what has actually happened."

She typed the reading for Sheila so that they could examine the words Gay had used for this woman. As Sandy typed, she could see that the dynamic between the fictional daughter and the wife was very much the same dynamic between the wife and the husband. Issues of power and freedom were the theme of the session. At one point, Gay even said to her, "I feel you would rather run away from this and yet you are being forced to deal with something here and it will be a great growing and learning experience for you." These were similar words to those given to her husband about her. She needed to stay and deal with their issues and he was forcing her to do that! Sandy tried to point this out to Sheila. Sheila was still unconvinced. Alan and Sandy suggested that Sheila let Gay address the problem:

"The energy I represent and bring forth is energy of God. I am here to give a perspective on the issues presented. I am not present to judge the so-called veracity of the material in terms of your physical reality. That is each individual's responsibility here. It is not my "job" nor am I interested in truth to be judged from that purely physical level. Now at issue here, indeed, is Sheila's perspective of what her work involves and who she is. It is important not to confuse what the role here of a trance channel is. Confusion begins when she adopts within her the definition of what a psychic is (as defined by others looking purely at the apparent evidence), and so a firm sense of who she is is important here and just what responsibility or nonresponsibility there is here. The sessions are not meant to be any more than a perspective, and anyone who chooses to be offended is not understanding their own personal power and deeper involvement in these sessions.

"For Sheila to let go of the idea that she is a "psychic" is important, for thinking of herself in these terms adds unnecessary pressure. A part of her feels that she is not performing well if she does not intuitively know every individual's questions and concerns without them telling her. Not only that, but she even ought to know their favorite dead great-uncle's middle name!

"Now, we from this perspective do not have this "knowledge." We are rather teaching a more general philosophy. I can only give my viewpoint based on the "facts" presented to me. Why should I do otherwise? It is you human entities who have determined that it must be otherwise. I am not speaking of you here right now, but of human entities in general, you understand. Now, I am clear in my, perhaps, vagueness, and I am much more concerned with channeling God energy on your planet than what is "ultimate truth." I feel that here is an opportunity to continue to love and to be firm in who you are. I am a friend and I am no more God than you are. It seems quite simple to me. Questions?"

(Could you describe the mechanism that occurs in a reading like this one, so that we can understand what happened?) "Now the presentation of the issue is presented and I can see the psychological/spiritual/mental energies brought with this individual and I simply apply this to the issues presented. I assume that the issue is "real" for they all are in truth "real." Here is this dispute. What is "reality"? Perhaps my definition is a bit too broad for some individuals. So be it. In that particular case, let me look closer. There is a daughter here and that is all I can actually say about this. I realize that this is not a defense, but you need no defense here. You are viewing reality differently. (In what way?) Differently than this person who came for this session. (Is the daughter on this line of physical reality?) The physical one you live in? Apparently not. Could be. (Could there be a daughter that the husband doesn't know about?) Possible, however, I feel more a strong probable existence. Perhaps she will look some day at her life thirteen years ago. (Why did Sheila draw this incident to her now?) She, Sheila, has asked to be a teacher to others. Sometimes this means through experiences rather than these sessions or classes. Now, of course, it is painful but I feel that, as I said, she needs to define what it is she does and what she represents. In truth, she is quite safe here now, and she can see through this to the love others have for her. In the physical plane, she forgets that there is love to draw upon through this event, friends are rallying, so to speak. It's bringing you all closer."

Sheila's participation in this seemingly terrible crisis of confidence was a necessary part of her own growth. The end result was a new, firmer relationship with Gay and a new understanding of the work she does.

The husband continued to have sessions with Gay and eventually he and his wife separated. Hopefully, someday she will look again at Gay's words and examine her own beliefs and actions with a different perspective.

Sheila's relationship with Gay is one of human in physical reality to non-physical entity in spiritual reality. These relationships are as influential as those between physical beings. We talked about "other selves" who exist on the earth plane during the same time period. In the session quoted above, Gay alludes to a "probable-self" of the wife. This brings up another kind of relationship that can indeed affect our reality. "Probable" selves are spin-offs from our present reality that "choose" a different path than the one we physically manifest. That is, they take a different probability than the one we take at any given moment. This concept is one that Sandy and Sheila learned about from Dick Sutphen and later read about in Jane Roberts' Seth books. Gay began talking of such selves at the beginning of the sessions and throughout the years they have cropped up at different times.

A young woman, we will call Dana, came with questions about her family. She was American born to European parents who had been emotionally unavailable, and sometimes even violent, during her growing years. She felt much anger about this and yet felt herself connected to them. She had recently undergone personal changes, becoming involved with a spiritual and metaphysical perspective that was influencing her to drop some old self-destructive behaviors. In two different sessions, Gay outlined the dramatic effects of her new choices:

"As to your family: They have been catalysts in your growth and you have "asked" for this experience, difficult as it is. You needed to struggle, and I feel you will one day feel a strong sense of power, having been through these experiences. You can develop a very strong sense of who you are and have empathy for others. Your situation is being used to a positive advantage for you. Think of this: A probable you has taken this same situation and is using some very harmful drugs. She is physically, emotionally, and psychically very unhealthy and is in the process of great deterioration. I feel that this probability is a real you even affecting you now. This probability lives in a large city and is lost in the world of drugs and bars. This has its effect on you. Give yourself credit for taking your same environment and using it to be all you are."

At the end of this session, Dana told Sandy and Sheila that while she was in college, she had experimented with drugs. She had also been thinking about moving to New York City to live but, instead, chose to remain in the Bucks County area where she subsequently met people who led her to spiritual pursuits. This, evidently, had been her "choice-point" which led to the creation of this other "probable self." In a later session, Gay went on to talk about the deeper implications this choice had on her spiritual growth:

"It is no accident that you are here in your present existence. This life is a transition for you, a life filled with dramatic contrasts and extreme changes and yet you wanted this to be for you needed to have all of this occur. From my perspective, life is beginning for you and you need to let go and accept the new life you have chosen. You could have died and then been reborn but you choose this particular way of change. Your probable self has died. I see a very violent death. This was one choice. You chose a new life but not in this way. You have chosen to allow yourself to open to love and this is painful in itself, for you have chosen a biological family that finds it difficult to open to love. I feel that you need to see that your purpose now is simply to concentrate on moving toward the light as though you have indeed died. Move now always toward the light. Allow the tears to fall as you leave the familiar; you will recognize the light, for it is warm and happy. Your whole being feels lighter. Move in this direction, for indeed you have died. I feel the death of this probable self also has, of course, influenced you. Her life is as "real" as the reality, you have chosen. Accustom yourself gradually to this new reality for it is another reality."

Dana's awareness of her relationship to a "probable" self, a probability not chosen by her currently focused physical self, leads her to a deeper understanding of her purpose in this lifetime. She came here to learn and to learn dramatically. She is now fully immersed in spiritual and metaphysical life as co-owner of a successful business and facilitator of New Age workshops.

All relationships—those on our physical plane and those that we consider "nonphysical"—are opportunities for us to expand our awareness of who we are and how rich and beautiful our multidimensional selves are. They are the stuff with which we create our ever-expanding realities.

Chapter XIV

Death as a Psychic Event of Life

Jaime's relationship with Betty developed gradually over the latter part of her first year and throughout her second year. Betty's kitchen window faced Sheila's living room window. As Betty puttered around her kitchen, Jaime would climb up on the chair and wave to her through the window. One of her first words was "Bet-tee." When Jaime started naming things, sometime around her second birthday, she would point at the different cars, chairs, personal belongings, whatever she could see and insist, "Mommy's car," "Daddy's chair," and so on. She would look at the house next door and declare, "Betty's house."

Two months after Jaime's second birthday, the 83-year-old Betty died. Her son came to tell Sheila and Alan of the viewing and so there was talk of Betty around the house during that day.

At bedtime, Sheila always took Jaime around her room so that she could say goodnight to all of her stuffed animals and the pictures on the wall. She and Alan were doing this the evening of the day that they had heard of Betty's death. Suddenly, Jaime looked over toward the door of her bedroom and brightened with a big smile. She reached out her arms and pursed her lips for a kiss. "Betty," she insisted. She repeated this several times, kissing and saying "Betty, Betty." Sheila and Alan could see no one there.

Jaime had had a special relationship with the old woman next door. There had been talk of her all through the day. Surely the thoughts and feelings in the house had "called" Betty there for a last good-bye to her little neighbor who had not lost the ability to perceive the realms where Betty now moved.

Pam dreamt that she was very sick and close to death. She lay in her old room in her parent's house. Her aunt came in through her bedroom window dressed in an army outfit. She crawled into the bed and pushed Pam out through the window. In the dream, Pam had a sense of switching places with her aunt so that she could live.

Shortly after this dream, Pam developed a malignant melanoma on her calf. She was immediately hospitalized and the melanoma and the lymph nodes in her groin were removed. While she was still groggy from the anesthesia, she overheard her parents talking about someone "not having much time to live." She thought that they were talking about her. Later she learned that her aunt had just been diagnosed with cancer and that the information had been held from her because of her health. Her aunt died a few days later.

Pam had not been particularly close to her aunt but her aunt was very close to her mother. Because of her dream, Pam has believed that the "switch" was made in order to save her mother the tremendous grief of losing a favored child.

Sandy's sister died unexpectedly at the early age of thirty-eight in 1979. Her sixteen-year-old daughter found her upon returning from school. The entire family was traumatized by the event but particularly this child. Sandy was at her father's house with the gathering family when her father called relatives in Florida to give them the news. Upon hearing the circumstances, her aunt gasped, "Oh, my God! That's what she has been talking about all day!"

Sandy's ninety-three-year-old senile grandmother lived in a nursing home in Florida. Her daughters visited her every day. During that particular day, starting sometime around eleven in the morning, she began repeating the same words over and over: "That poor child, finding her mother that way!" Sandy's niece found her mother about two-thirty that afternoon. Evidently, her grandmother had been traveling through time and space and had witnessed the event before it happened in our time sequence. Sandy's father turned to her and said, "This one's for you!" He, of course, was referring to her interest in psychic happenings.

Psychic events around a death are common and each family has its own story. Sometimes, however, the events involve people distant from one's immediate circle of loved ones. It seems that some of us are drawn into these events for our learning or, perhaps, even to be of help.

During the night of January 12, 1982, both Sheila and Sandy's fourteen-year-old son Steven, dreamt of a plane crash. On January 13, a plane did crash in Washington, D.C., killing eighty-one people. Both Sheila and Steven were extremely disturbed by this event. This had happened before, and Gay had told both of them that they were "helpers" during sleep and went to victims to aid their transition from physical life to spirit realms. This explanation had been interesting and had helped them understand their distress. This time, Gay volunteered some information the day after the event, on January 14th:

"I wish to comment that some individuals involved in the plane crash are around you asking for some help. They are quite confused. A tiny baby is looking for its mother. This was a very sad and abrupt situation. (Steven's been asking about this crash. Is he picking up on this?)

"Yes, very much. Both he and Sheila are inundated with requests for help. Perhaps he needs to know. He could most help the baby."

On January 15th, the *Philadelphia Inquirer* ran a human interest piece about the plane crash: "Priscilla Tirado, who doctors said came nearer death than any other survivor of the airplane crash in the Potomac River, has learned her husband and two-month-old son are dead." This article was the first information printed about the death of an infant.

Steven became emotionally involved with another tragic event involving the death of children three years later. On a Saturday evening, he was driving to the

Jersey shore where he was to spend the night and the next day visiting a girl-friend and her family. Still in Trenton, New Jersey, driving off a major highway on to a city street, he witnessed an automobile accident. The car directly in front of him, driving too fast to make the transition from highway to local street, flew out of control and off the road into some trees. Steve stopped and ran to the car to help but a policeman arrived at the same time that he did. He backed off so as not to be in the way, however, he saw the entire scene. Two young, black boys had been thrown out of the car on to the pavement. Steve thought they were about five or six years old. He could see the driver of the car, and believed the driver to be a man.

One boy was dead and the other screamed and flopped "all over the road," his head crushed. The driver of the car seemed to be okay and kept trying to get up but the policeman would not allow that. The car was up in a tree, upside down, bent in half, like an accordian.

It is always traumatic to witness an accident involving death; however, this time Steven's emotional response and his perceptions of the event raised some interesting questions about our interactions with others on psychic planes. Steve was unable to continue on his way to the shore for a long time after the bodies were removed and the accident site cleared. He sat and cried for about an hour before resuming his trip. He said that he felt an "overwhelming attachment" to the two boys and extreme anger toward the "father," who he assumed was driving the car. He wanted to help but felt helpless. "I wanted to bring that little boy back to life," he later cried to Sandy on the phone, "and I couldn't. They were just perfect little boys, so beautiful." He also raged at the "father," "I didn't care about him. I was so angry at him. He must have been traveling 100 miles an hour to do what he did to that car!"

All that night he thought about the accident. He talked to his girlfriend about it. When he arrived home on Sunday night, he was extremely irritated and refused the dinner that Sandy offered him. When she pushed him to talk about what was bothering him, he broke down and cried again, telling her a second time how much he cared for the boys and how much he hated the "father." "I felt so connected to those little boys," he kept saying.

Sandy suggested that perhaps he was there on the scene for a reason and that his presence and emotions may have helped the boys because he cared about them. She urged him to consciously ask his dream self to help during sleep that night.

The next day, the local newspaper carried the story. The driver of the car was a woman. Her son died. The other boy was a friend and he survived. The boys were nine and eleven years old. Sandy was struck by inconsistencies between Steven's perceptions of the players in this drama and the actual facts. She wondered whether or not her sensitive, psychic son was picking up on a past-life event in which he had been more closely involved with these people and perceiving according to this past? Sometimes emotional "overlays" from one lifetime to another cause us to not perceive the actual physical events here. The emotional reality, however, remains intact and powerful.

Events surrounding another tragic automobile accident turned around the life of one of Sandy and Sheila's closest friends. Tom was a young man who habitually swung between two extremes. The first was a rigid, monastic lifestyle with hours of meditation and a strict, ascetic diet which included absolutely no chemicals. The second phase would involve hours of drinking, daily pot smoking, and a poor diet with subsequent weight gain. Tom did not know what he wanted in life. He was attracted to spiritual ideas and frequently would make decisions that he should be a certain way, judging that his past lifestyle was "bad," then adopting an extremely austere way of living. He then would become tired of the lonely life of an ascetic, deciding that he wanted to "live." That would begin a new bout of alcohol and drugs. During these times, he would judge himself severely and talk about wanting to die.

Early in 1981, he and two of his buddies were on a binge. They had been drinking most of the day and were playing cards about seven-thirty at night when someone suggested that they go out to a bar. They planned to leave at about eight. About a quarter to eight, Tom was struck with a severe headache. He describes it as the worst headache that he has ever had. He could hardly move. This was unusual because he was not normally prone to headaches of any kind. He told the others to go ahead. They agreed to return for him at a later hour. They left and he fell asleep.

He was awakened at three in the morning by a loud banging on the door. It was the police. His friends had died instantly in one of the worst automobile accidents in Bucks County history. Five or six young people in the second car also died.

A few days later, Tom called Sandy. "I have to talk about this. It makes no sense. I wanted to die. They didn't. It's not fair. It's obvious that something protected me."

Sandy suggested that he come and talk to Gay. A couple of months later, he did. He was still angry and confused. Gay's opening words reflected his mood at the time:

"Your remark, "this is enough of negativity" is quite significant. You might say it is a clue to a deeper way of relating, for actually this "negativity" you express tonight is simply energy. This energy needs to be felt and expressed to its fullest, for there is tremendous power in this energy. The very thing you have been asking for comes with this energy. The energy is the beauty, and you are the beauty of energy expressing itself.

"All the events you have drawn to yourself were specifically designed to bring forth this energy. The events, of course, in particular, the accident, were "destined" to occur anyway. The participants have their own reasons for their involvement. Your involvement is a part of feeling the energy that you are feeling tonight. It is your key to the freedom you asked for. You cannot ask without receiving and the door is opening. Do not block these energies even by labeling them negative, for you have asked to be free and they are the key to what you want. As you become clear about what you want, it indeed comes to pass. Death is not what you want for there is a deep belief in life. There is also a need to continue to struggle, but this is ending. The accident has been a shock to your psyche and your physical being. The physical self needs time to recover from this event. I feel that you may need to rest and simply be aware that your physical body too is in a state of change. The psyche also needs to rest, but you needed to have this drama. Otherwise, you had been content to struggle. That sounds like a paradox but it is indeed true. The anger you feel is a tremendous catalyst for higher energies, and I suggest simply recognizing that this is a form of energy."

Gay then went on to discuss Tom's two friends and their reasons for choosing death in this way. This event, these feelings and their subsequent energy did prove to be the turning point in Tom's life. He began to ask to know what he wanted for his life. He changed the "swing" pattern in which he had been caught. He found a balance between his spiritual leanings and his need to be with people. When he asked "I wanted to die, so why them and not me?" he began to realize that he did have a purpose in his life. Years later, he told Sandy that it was then that he began to perceive "life as a gift."

Tom is now married and has two beautiful children. He has found work that he enjoys and has been extremely successful in a relatively short period of time. He still struggles occasionally but more and more he finds the balance and harmony in his life that he had been unconsciously asking for when he was hit with that "blinding headache."

Gay had said that the participants in the accident had "their own reasons for their involvement." Tom later asked why his friends chose to die in this way:

"Ray is a guide but realized that he set many seemingly impossible conditions in his present life—that were barriers to what he wanted to do, and so death was his desire. He wanted death much more than you did. Your work is in your present life. His is now in spirit and so you must trust. Bob "chose" death because he did not want a particular responsibility that his father felt was his. This was his way of saying no, rather dramatically, but each person does what they want ultimately."

The idea that we all "choose" our death is often unsettling to people of our Western culture who have always perceived death as a threat, as something outside of our control, something that comes and takes us over, something in which we have no power or say. As we begin to be aware that we are indeed the creators of our reality, then we must also take responsibility for all of that reality including its seeming end. Some of us are even conscious of that "final choice."

A beautiful, young woman came for a session with Gay. She had had a long, intermittent relationship with a man who had just died. This man had disappeared from her life for months at a time, then suddenly reappeared in the middle of the night. She suspected that he lived a wild life and she heard that he had died on railroad tracks. Gay talked at length about his sensitivity and his difficulties in past lives with that sensitive nature. He needs to "accept" that part of himself, she insisted, but rather than accept, he rebelled, deciding to "fight" the world even though he deeply wanted to relax. She continued:

"You are already aware that Joey did indeed decide on his death. Perhaps not the exact moment consciously, but he was much more conscious of this process than most individuals. And because of this, he is quite aware of his death and he does not regret leaving his physical body. He did not wish to be old, primarily because in his belief system old is associated with being weak and losing his physical powers. This was something that he could not tolerate."

Joey's refusal to accept his sensitivity and his belief that old is weak led to his early, conscious decision to leave physical life. Sometimes, as in the case of Pam and her aunt, the choice is made to help another.

Keri came for a session with Gay and asked about her father's death. She was puzzled by this death because it had always been her mother who was sick. Everyone in the family expected her mother to die. She suffered with heart disease for years. She and her husband had been very close, however, and in many ways he depended upon her for basic needs. He had been a military man, she his valet. She waited on him, even laying out his clothes each morning before he dressed. Gay's touching words demonstrate how he chose to express his gratitude:

"He wants your mother with him. He is calling her to be with him. I feel that his energy is strong and that he wanted to make contact with her. I feel that he wanted to die so that he could help her to make the transition. I feel that he did this to be there for her. It was, in a sense, planned, although not consciously, you understand? I feel that in many ways, it is safer now for your mother to permit herself to die, although this may not necessarily happen soon. I feel it was a kind of pact between them. Your mother had much more fear about death than your father. He decided to take care of her in this way. To your mother, I would suggest that you simply tell her that, yes, he was present for her and remains close. He is helping her to understand the different reality. I do not feel that she would understand right now the "decision" he made to die but death is always a decision at some level."

Sandy's father died of cancer at the age of 65. This event was a shock to the entire family because the members of this family usually lived well into their nineties. He had suffered digestive discomfort for years and finally decided to do something about it, so in September he had entered the hospital for a routine gall bladder operation. The hospital required the standard chest X-ray upon admission. The radiologist found a spot on his lungs. Sandy's father insisted that it was "nothing," a shadow which had been there for years. The doctors insisted that there was cause for investigation. In three weeks time, Sandy's father underwent three different operations. He had lung cancer.

Sandy was devastated. She could not understand why he was choosing this at this time in his life. He had retired from his business just two years earlier and seemed to enjoy his present lifestyle, spent mostly on Florida's golf courses. He and his present wife had bought a home on the East coast of Florida near his retired sisters. They seemed to have a happy and varied social life.

Sandy did not know her new stepmother well. She seemed like a nice woman, but while staying with her in Florida during the weeks of her father's operations, Sandy began to see some interactions that were disturbing. This wife was extremely dependent upon her father, even to the point of carrying simple concerns like whether to wash the car into the intensive care unit of the hospital for her father's decision. Sandy could not imagine that her father, who was extremely independent and had sired strong and powerful daughters, would like this kind of behavior.

Upon her return home, she had a channeled session with Ginny Ramus who speaks for the guide, Valoos. She asked about her father's health. Valoos explained that her father was in the process of making a decision. A large part of him wanted to leave physical life to be with Ellie, his previous wife of twenty years, who had died fifteen years ago. Sandy knew that he had loved Ellie very much and had suspected that he missed her. Valoos then said that Ellie was urging him to stay and "finish business with Linda." Linda was his present wife. "What could that possibly mean?" Sandy thought.

He recovered from the surgery and returned home, undergoing chemotherapy over the next several months. Sandy visited him again in December, this time with her family. He told her that he had never felt better in his life. He looked great. He and Linda were planning to move further north to Central Florida. "It's less congested there," he explained, "and less expensive to live."

They moved sometime around March. As he always did, Sandy's father puttered around their new home, fixing this and creating that. In June, they were to come North to Pennsylvania for a visit, then continue on to Vermont to visit Sandy's sister.

Three weeks before they were due to arrive, Sandy received a call. He was back in the hospital. She called his doctor, a woman cancer specialist in whom he had great confidence. She, the doctor, was crying. "I don't know what happened," she said. "Two weeks ago, he looked almost clear. Very little signs of tumor. Now it has spread throughout his body, even into his bones. I don't think he will live two months."

Taken by surprise, Sandy and her sister decided to drive to Florida. They did not know how long they would be there. Their father had insisted on going home, and a hospital bed with oxygen had been brought in for what everyone expected to be a couple of months at the very least. Sandy and Gail arrived on a Saturday night. He was awake and waiting for them. He asked about their families, then sent them to bed. He stayed awake all night in spite of the large amounts of pain and sleep medications that he was taking. When the sun came up, he fell asleep. By eleven that morning, his sisters and brother-in-law had arrived. His entire family was there with him. About eleven-thirty, he died peacefully with each of his daughters speaking in his ears, giving him their love and support.

The ambulance arrived to take him to the hospital. Sandy jumped in the back with him because she knew that Linda, who was riding in the front and was not aware that he had actually died, would be upset. She continued to talk to him in her mind. Half way to the hospital, she was overtaken by a strong, joyful feeling and the words "I did it the way I wanted" popped into her mind. Upon arriving at the hospital, she learned that her sister had the same experience at the same time while riding in the car following the ambulance. They cried together, their grief mingled with joy because they knew that their father had sent them a message.

Later that day, Sandy's uncle found a note in the utility room where her father had kept his tools. It was a list of projects that he was completing on the new house. The last one was the only one not crossed off. Linda explained that they had been on their way to buy the overhead fan that she had wanted when he collapsed and had to be taken to the hospital. Sandy knew now what "finishing business with Linda" had meant. He had always been a man who did things his own way, neat and precise. He chose to live his death as he had lived his life.

Sometimes the choosing of death is more obviously apparent. When people choose suicide, we know that they are consciously determining their own destiny even though that kind of decision brings an intense pain to surviving family members and friends. Somehow that kind of decision is less "acceptable" than dying of "natural causes." If we create our own reality, choosing our birth and our death, then all death is suicide. We need to learn that the dynamics of this kind of choice are often the same as "unconscious" decisions.

Sheila and Sandy's good friend, Margaret, learned that her mother had killed herself. Although she had known for years that her mother was depressed and unhappy, she was still shocked by the event, much of her own fear and pain triggered by her mother's decision. She talked to Gay who discussed the effects of suicide on both the person choosing death and on those that remain in physical life:

"Through this event there is learning for you of your own strength and of your power. The same power that runs the universe runs through you and is you. You forget at times the perspective of God As You. You forget that God is All That Exists, and that is all you need to know right now. You are reacting to a very real event that indeed is painful and you are allowing yourself to open to the feelings of this event. Your mother's reality (which is always of the mind) has not altered that much. Yes, the focus is in a different realm; however, the issues are still the same. Her learning is that the direction she took does not alter her inner reality. It's much like what often occurs when someone moves to another location thinking that will solve the dilemma. That is all she needs to learn here. In one sense, she took an action even though not understanding fully what this meant. Your mother is having to face some issues, surprised that she is not instantly blissful without problems. But she is with guides and towards you love flows easier than on the physical plane where she was afraid to openly and physically express love. I feel that you need to allow yourself to be as you are, seeing at the same time that power is in the present moment."

Margaret asked if her mother had felt powerful when she made the conscious decision to die. And if so, was that important to her?

"She did, yes. Of course it was very important to her. You need to recognize that no matter what you may hear or read in the future about this kind of dying, death, as life, is still individual and unique. There is no horrible punishment or karma but what the individual soul needs. Your mother is simply quietly reviewing her life and interacting with some souls that she has known in other existences. She's wondering why the euphoria is gone and she feels a bit powerless. Perhaps we can teach her on this level of her power also. Your task now is to be aware of your power. I feel this is indeed an important step along a process for you of being aware of your wholeness once again."

Margaret was indeed learning about her power and her mother's choice did push her along with this learning. She was struggling with a mysterious and debilitating illness at the time of her mother's death. Five years later she has learned wellness and is now using her creative talents to help others deal with their chronic illnesses.

The death of a young man gave Gay an opportunity to explore in depth the interactions between our beliefs and how we live and die. Addie was only twenty-six when she came to Mind Matters. Her twenty-seven year old husband had just died. She was suffering grief mixed with guilt as we often do in these circumstances. She felt that she had not done enough, that she had not loved him enough, given him enough. As she talked about Greg, Sandy and Sheila got a picture of a withdrawn, scared young man who was afraid to be close. Addie felt as though she ought to have been able to reach him but failed. In fact, just before he died she was thinking about leaving him. That added immensely to her guilt. In Gay's words, we can see some of their interaction and much of his personal belief system:

"Many individuals would like to think that because someone has died they are suddenly omniscient and that they have power not usually apparent in everyday life. They suddenly increase in stature and the consensus among the living is that they want to communicate. This is not always so. Each individual is as unique in death as in life. I can begin with this premise so that you can better understand this situation and how you fit into this event, how and why you drew these circumstances into your life. Greg has not changed in death. He does not want to communicate and he has his back turned to others. He, in truth, is much more sensitive than he wants anyone to see. It took great energy to keep this hidden and not letting others see his emotions was a large preoccupation with him. He succeeded quite well and often frustrated you with this withdrawal. I feel that throughout his life, he felt that no one would ever understand anyway so he did not try. Even though he knew you would, it was too painful by then to risk being so vulnerable, and so he worked at protecting himself with a kind of psychic wall. This wall, though, prevented necessary healing energies from reaching him, and he did not believe that anyone wanted to help him. In a sense, his death was this statement.

"He realizes his death and is angry about its occurrence, for he feels cheated but that was his feeling anyway for a long time. He has yet to realize his own participation in bringing this about and so he is not communicating. He does, however, occasionally make his presence known and those times he just wants to remind you that he is aware of you. He does not want you to forget him. He does not want you with anyone else. Of course, you already know this, and you can deal with this by being aware. It will, I feel, help you in your spiritual and emotional growth to deal with this. He is so much more transparent than he wishes. This makes him somewhat angry too. As I look at him, he is angry because I am speaking to you. I feel that he was not aware of how he died; and although in dreams there was vast preparation, it came as a surprise consciously, for in his conscious mind, he thought he could overcome anything and so this contributes to the frustration."

Gay then talked to Addie about her feelings of guilt that she had not done enough. She assured Addie that she had given all that she could. She described Greg's need for love but also his strong belief that he could not have it. This made him unable to accept what Addie offered to him. His fear of rejection would take over and he would push her away. Finally, Gay discussed one of the basic beliefs behind his death. Speaking of Addie's desire to love Greg, she continued:

"His fear set in, yet you persisted. You might not have continued had he lived, and this was his fear, yet he was slowly bringing the fear into reality. In another way, too, his death was his chance to leave you before you could leave him. That sounds ridiculous but sometimes people think in ridiculous ways. You understand this but do not feel it was your fault, for this is simply his belief system and he needs to learn how to accept love."

Five months after this initial session, Addie returned to talk to Gay a second time about Greg. There had been some changes:

"He does indeed come to you in your dreams. They are the primary source of communication and I feel that you need to program yourself, perhaps through hypnosis, to remember more of these dreams and to write them down for there are messages that you can receive when the time is right. You can receive messages for his family. The time is not yet right for this kind of message. You are the one that I feel can channel these messages, but you must trust what you receive and you must write down upon awakening the impressions that you receive. He is most likely to communicate first to you than to others for he is aware of your belief in consciousness surviving death. He was not always so certain of this concept himself and to have his consciousness survive came as a surprise. There are still some adjustments to be made in this reality."

Greg had become softer during this time. He still was somewhat distant but was attempting dream communication. He still had some anger, mostly directed now at those who are still in physical bodies and are healthy. Gay spoke of his need to keep his feelings to himself and how much energy that took in the last months of his illness. Now, however, he is concerned about his mother and headaches that she has been having. Gay continued to urge Addie to be open to "messages" for his family. Learning continues on spiritual planes and eventually Greg could learn "how to accept love."

All deaths offer opportunities for learning. There is nothing, however, that brings more emotional intensity to human beings than the loss of a child. Ginny and Tracy, Sandy and Sheila's closest friends, experienced a summer of incredible loss that brought with it intense learning. Ginny and Tracy are both spiritually and psychically aware, having studied and worked in metaphysical areas for years. During the summer of 1984, they had been married a couple of years, and had an eighteen-month-old daughter, Julia. Ginny was pregnant with their second child.

Early in the summer, Ginny became concerned about Julie's left eye. It appeared "lazy," drifting off to one side. Julia would rub it, complaining that it hurt. Ginny and Tracy took her to the pediatrician who sent them immediately to Children's Hospital in Philadelphia. Julia had eye cancer and had to have her eye removed. For weeks, everyone close to the family meditated and prayed for Julia. There was a danger than the cancer could have spread to both eyes or into her brain.

Then in the middle of a July night, Julia woke screaming. Ginny and Tracy were puzzled by this as it had never happened before. Ten minutes later, overdue by a few days, Ginny went into what appeared to be labor, but it came with blood and severe cramps.

They called Sandy and Sheila who rushed over to help. Sheila stayed with Julia while Sandy drove them to the hospital. She and Tracy sat outside the operating room holding hands and praying while doctors and nurses ran back and forth shouting for blood. The baby was dead. Ginny was weak but she lived. The nurses came and asked Tracy if Ginny should see the baby. "She's a beautiful, perfect little girl," the seasoned nurse said, tears in her eyes.

Tracy was reluctant. He wanted to protect Ginny from pain. Sandy knew that if it were her, she would have to see the baby in order to believe it was true. She gently urged Tracy to give permission. He did and the nurses brought the baby into the room with Ginny. Around her were Tracy, Sandy, and her father-in-law. She held the baby, a beautiful little girl they named Eliza, examining her, touching each part of her, turning her, caressing her, loving her. The moment was intensely painful, yet exquisitely beautiful and loving. It was essential to Ginny, to know her daughter and accept her death.

During several conversations that Ginny and Tracy shared with Sandy shortly after Eliza's death, several psychic influences became apparent. First of all, Julia awakening just before Ginny's pain seemed important to Tracy. Driving home from the hospital, the next day, he told Sandy that he felt that Eliza was a "trade" for Julia. He and Ginny had been having a difficult time feeling ready for a second child so soon after Julia's illness. Tired as he was, almost in a trance-like state, he talked about "knowing" that Julia had been deciding whether to live or die. Now he felt that she would live. Interestingly, over the subsequent years,

Julia has continued to talk about the lost baby, sometimes crying because she wants her sister to be alive or wanting to be dead herself so that she could be with Eliza.

While Ginny was on the operating table, drifting off with the anesthesia, she remembered a dream that she had had weeks before. In the dream, a woman from her childbirth classes named Julie had a Caesarean section and the baby was born dead because her uterus was filled with "fluid." She remembered the dream because one of the nurses called her Julie. Her response to remembering the dream was different than we might logically presume since she wanted so very much for her baby to live. Rather than feel frightened, she immediately felt peaceful, accepting that it was "right." During all of this thought process, Ginny felt herself out of the physical body, somewhere up and above what was happening on the operating table.

Tracy had a similar experience at the same time. While he and Sandy sat outside, listening to all the drama going on down the hall—nurses running back and forth as doctors shouted for blood—he suddenly got a sense that Ginny could die. Again, rather than being scared, he felt peaceful. He knew that it would be okay if he and Julia were left alone together.

Later when they compared experiences, Ginny and Tracy realized that somehow they had "met" on some emotional and psychic level, him feeling the peace that Ginny had because of her preparatory dream. This feeling of peace remained extremely important to them both through the weeks and months of grieving and healing that lay ahead of them.

Both of the parents learned from their loss. Before Eliza's birth and death, Tracy had been an overly strict, almost tyrannical father to Julia. He had definite ideas about how she should be raised and often criticized Ginny for being too "soft" with Julia. Julia's illness and Eliza's death brought about deep changes in him. Instead of worrying about discipline, he began concentrating on love, appreciating Julia in a way in which he had not been capable before these events.

Ginny faced some deep fears within herself. She had always been afraid of doing the "wrong" thing. A few weeks after the event, she said to Sandy, "I am learning that I did not do anything 'wrong,' that what has happened is 'right' and as it should have happened. I realize that all the people who come around and tell me what I should have done or not done, triggering my old usual guilt feelings are doing just that, triggering old feelings. I am learning that I did not have to do something wrong for these events to have occurred."

Part of Ginny's learning then was that *she* did not do anything wrong and her sense of "rightness" of the events, illogical as they may seem on the surface, brought about a wonderful leap in her learning and spiritual growth.

Two years later Ginny and Tracy decided to have another child. Before making love, they meditated and invited Eliza to come back into their lives as a boy. She conceived and nine months later Luke was born, easily and lovingly accepted into their family.

Carrie and Robert came to see Sheila to talk to Gay. This couple had a calm energy about them, so when Sandy and Sheila heard their story, they knew that immense learning was taking place. Carrie and Robert had three children. The oldest, a girl, suffered with cerebral palsy. The boys were twins, born with congenital cancer. The first boy died at a year and a half. The second twin had just died at age five. Gay's words lead us into a dimension of learning that none of us would consciously choose, yet this young couple had:

"These children, that we might call yours, are and have been in other lifetimes, your teachers. Teachers often assume many roles, many disguises in order for you to grow and to understand love and experience love at many different levels. You are not being punished here even in any karmic sense. Rather you "volunteered" to learn some very important spiritual concepts and to accept and embrace all of what being alive is. For you both there has been, in your present existence and in other lifetimes, a tendency to deny pain, to deny anger, and these so-called negative emotions. These emotions are a part of who you are and expressing them is expressing the God Within You. It is most important to fully experience now the inner grief and rage at the universe, even toward God. This is, as you both know, a very healthy response; however, your tendency is to not want to bother anyone with this, and yet, in a sense, you cannot move without acknowledging this and, of course, I feel there is opportunity and potential to open to each other at a much deeper level than you have thought possible in the past. I feel that you are both teachers and I feel that there is a great deal of sharing to be done with others but that is a distance away, and, of course, always involves your own choices.

"Now, as I said, all of your children have been teachers in other lives. I see that you both struggled with the concept of justice from a universal standpoint, not understanding and wanting to know why such tragedy can occur in human existence. I feel that you have had to experience this to become closer to who you truly are. You are being taught a lesson also in love, and it is often through feeling such deep rage that you can accept that there is love. There is also a need to allow yourselves to give and receive love without holding on tightly. You have been together, the two of you, in other lives and I see Alan [the five year old who just died] teaching you at the time of Christ, soon after Christ's death. I see you both wanting, in a sense, to possess this teacher, to never allow him to be away from you and not being accepting when he said it was time to leave, even though reminding you of great love. In your present existence, you have shared a great deal with this same entity, this same being. I also feel this being very attached to his brother, an entity who simply has a great deal of difficulty being in physical reality at all. There are lessons for this being to learn and yet he resists. Alan was, in a sense, pulled toward helping him and knowing at this deeper level that he had given you a great deal and through leaving was also teaching you a great deal. This is not so easy to see at times, and you must accept that this is difficult and let it be difficult."

Carrie and Robert were learning how to let go, how to feel what ever may be there, difficult as it is. Their children were their teachers, with them for a time in order to bring about the learning they "volunteered" to undertake. Letting go is one of the most difficult lessons that we learn in this physical existence. Gay reassured this couple that their son, Alan, "remains close to you both. This being remains near you and yet had to leave. I feel that you can trust a presence of love around you."

What happens when this letting go does not occur? Sandy and Sheila had an opportunity to experience a situation in which the holding on to a dead child was so severe that the intense, psychic atmosphere surrounding those involved was stifling. A good friend of Irwin and Mary asked if Sheila and Sandy would go with him to their home in order to hold a session about their daughter, Linda. Linda had died at the age of seventeen about six years earlier. The friend thought that she had drowned but was not sure because Irwin and Mary refused to talk about the death. He felt that perhaps a session with Gay would help this couple release the hold this event had on their lives. The extent of that hold was evident as soon as Sandy and Sheila arrived.

The home was lovely, filled with beautiful artifacts from around the world. This couple traveled extensively and operated an importing business in the area. As the two women were led through the house to see the art collection, they began to notice photographs of Linda placed among the rich, profuse variety of sights. Photographs on every wall, in every room. Finally, they reached a bedroom, perfectly made up for a teenage girl, complete with stuffed animals, a cluttered dresser, frilly bedspread and curtains, and soft pink lighting. Then, in the room where the session was to occur, they saw a large picture of Linda with candles around it and the word "love" embroidered on a tapestry draped across the top of the photograph. Sandy felt that it was a shrine.

Mary and Irwin were very secretive at first, hinting at their concerns, never mentioning the daughter's death. They had talked about her while walking throughout the house but it was as if she were simply away for a while. Gay opened the session by describing their present state of mind:

"You have many, many questions but, of course, you wait for the biggest question. Can you trust? How much should you reveal of yourselves? Your skepticism is quite natural and it is a healthy form of protection, for you are in many ways far more open than you consciously wish that you were. There is a looking back to the past and yet a yearning to be satisfied in the now, but you are clinging to the past."

She then talked to them about their relationship, particularly mentioning Irwin's tendency to protect Mary. It was then that the barriers broke and Sandy and Sheila learned the extent of that "protection." Mary finally asked about Linda. As soon as she did, Sheila began to feel tremendous pressure in her ears and hear music in the background. Sandy too felt extreme pressure in her ears and soon the room began to undulate around her. She asked how Linda died. Mary said that she could not talk about it, shaking her head, her fist in her mouth. Gay began to speak:

"Letting go of pressure is very difficult. It always has been here though hidden. This pressure is quite real and it involves performing, for you believed you had to be perfect parents, and she thought she had to be perfect also, perfect for her friends and then perfect at home. But this was not one-sided and you must let go of guilt, for you, in particular, Mary, wanted to be a perfect mother.

"In many prior lifetimes, there were attempts to have children and you were not able to. You did not trust in yourself but you also felt that you must have done something wrong. Music was a part of her life and I feel this quite strongly. I do feel and hear this music. You do need, however, to let go and allow yourself to feel the job of living now. Linda remains strongly with you and yet she must also go free as must you both. You have each been with her before. Mary, she was once your mother and you ran away from her. You suffered because you felt responsible for illnesses that later developed. This influences the excessive responsibility that you feel now. You, of course, need to believe in the closeness and to trust more.

"There are no accidents even among the very young. What often appears as an accident is more planned (subconsciously) than you realize. This was a realization that something was indeed finished here. Pressure was intense among friends and she did not want to make choices. In many ways this was the easiest solution. You must know that there is love and let go. See what you have now. There has been a fear until now of hearing what I say or seeing what is here now. You have much to give to each other even though you may doubt this at times. Let go and find who you are now. Realize that you can give strength to each other now. There is peacefulness beyond death. You simply are all stuck in a certain perspective. Linda is not what you could think of as unhappy. She is, however, psychically attempting to reassure you that you can all let go, particularly of guilt. As I explained, choices are made but that does not imply unhappiness. Often it simply means that what has happened is finished and it is time to move away. The pressure was indeed there, but also there are lessons in simply letting go and accepting change. Linda was willing to do both and she wishes to teach you this. While alive she was willing to accept that life means change. Death was no different than simply moving away, and it was not seen as a horrible catastrophe, for she is quite aware that the bonds still exist."

After these words, Mary began to talk. She had been feeling guilty for years about her daughter's death. When it occurred, she was so distraught that Irwin wanted to protect her from more pain and ordered the funeral to be completed before Mary was ready and could attend. She never saw her dead daughter. "This is the first time that I have said out loud that my daughter is dead," she declared.

Sandy thought to herself that all of the pressure that she and Sheila had felt was this girl screaming to be free. The pressure was psychic. Linda had never even lived in this house, they now learned. She had died in New York a couple of years before Irwin and Mary moved to Pennsylvania. She had had pressure during life to be perfect and now the pressure was on her to be there when she was not. It was time indeed for everyone involved to let go.

Margaret's dog, Ivan, was a spirited being. He loved to explore and, much to her distress, would often run off, visiting neighbors. Often a phone call from a concerned neighbor sent Margaret out the door to collect her errant adventurer who had been investigating new territory and making new friends. Ivan feared nothing. He was friendly and persistent, taking off any time he could grab the opportunity. Then the day came when he was killed, hit by a car. Margaret was devastated by his loss and came to talk to Gay who puts death into a perspective that sees it as part of life:

"Ivan continues to teach even in his death. It is true from a certain perspective that death is a choice that is made by each individual, but the choice is not necessarily a choice against life or against love, for in the reality in which you exist, death is an integral part of life itself. There is much to learn about death but it is seemingly an inescapable part of life itself and is not a rejection of life. Certainly it was not in this case at all. Death was as much a shock to Ivan as to you, for he trusted totally in each moment and while this is a beautiful quality, it does indeed leave open many alternatives, each being equally acceptable to this dog's consciousness. Animals do indeed have a consciousness. He does not view death as even a separation. This consciousness sees no distinction. At least not now, perhaps because of the suddenness, but I also feel it to be simply an exploration like many of his explorations. I feel that he naturally assumes you are still together. He is playing as an errant child who foolishly wants to explore. Of course, the foolishness is in our judgment, it is far from foolish, but his exploring was with no thoughts as to what has happened. In truth, I feel the separateness is in your mind.

"Of course the physical separateness is quite real and cannot be denied. Your physical being feels this physical loss, and indeed at this level there is a great void and a loss. Time indeed heals this grief. Although you have heard this many times, still you judge yourself foolish for feeling so strongly over an animal. You know you have the right to do so, but your surrounding culture is very cut off from nature and these feelings. Ivan teaches you, of course, to let go and love all the ways he chooses to explore. He did not foresee a physical separation. He may realize this and mourn it in his own way, but in many respects animals learn quicker and with your permission he would like to rejoin with you. It is up to you. Ivan had so much energy he could not stop and went fast into new explorations. It was his way. He loved life and so, of course, loved his experience of death."

As we begin to realize our multidimensional nature, we may begin to accept life and death as Ivan did—a grand exploration and opportunity to learn!

Chapter XV

Summing Up

What is it all about? Why should we know all of this? Life is complicated enough without having to know all this subtle, invisible stuff going on around us! If we are aware of all this "karma" with its past life influences and telepathic implications, then we have even more to deal with in our lives. It's too much!

Indeed! We do live in our present and our present is where we need to focus in order to create full and joyful lives. If, however, we can imagine our present as the point in the pool where the stone falls, then we can see how the choices we make in our present ripple throughout our being, affecting the entire pool. Throw in many, many stones, each one rippling outward, the waves overlapping one another in every direction, then we can imagine the wonderful complexity and dynamic nature of our reality. We throw the stones, creating the ripples, some are great waves, others less noticeable. The more awareness we have of these ripples and waves, the more say we have in the texture and depth of our pool.

We have been learning about relationships and the effects of others' stones on our pool. Ultimately, all pools interconnect and feed into one huge ocean of consciousness. Our business, however, is to clean and maintain our own pool, creating the clearest, deepest, most harmonious body of water possible. In order to do that, we need to expand our awareness of how our pool, with its ripples and waves, works.

We are the creators of our reality. We determine who and what influences our choices, our lives. If indeed we are affected by an event from a past life, or the thoughts and feelings of another person, or our own deep beliefs, then it is in our best interest as creators to determine our own participation in what is happening. Others influence us only when we allow it. Likewise, we influence others only when they allow it. This is very important to realize. Often humans feel and behave like victims, blaming others for their reality; or they take on too much responsibility for the reality of others, suffering tremendous guilt unnecessarily. Again, it is awareness of these influences which ultimately brings freedom to choose, freedom to create consciously.

What can you do once you know about an influence? The first step is to recognize that you are participating in what is happening. That recognition gives you power. When you know that on some level or another you are "co-creating" events, as well as your own responses to others, then you have the power to change how you respond to others in your life and change what events you draw into your life.

The next step involves asking yourself *what* you want in the situation. Most people know what they do not want, particularly in relationships. Consciously creating a vision of what you want in your life is one of the most important steps you will ever take. Make a list of qualities, concentrate on concretely knowing what those qualities mean to you and how you will know that you have them in your life when they appear. Indeed, they will appear. We always get what we concentrate on, but what we concentrate on is usually what we do not want.

Next, ask yourself what stops you from having what you want. You may be surprised that you know more about that than you think you do. However, here is where it becomes important to dive deeper into your pool. Seek out practitioners who have the methods to take you deep within yourself. You may need to undergo a past-life regression or a series of regressions in order to find the deeper influences in your life. You can do this without outside help; however, most people find that guidance and support aids their investigations. A qualified past-life regressionist who has been trained in metaphysics and psychology can offer immeasurable help.

Our reality is dynamic; the stones cast by our consciousness in an all-encompassing Now, overlap and interact with one another. Remembering this, we can begin to realize just how we have the power to heal our past. When we reach out to a past-life self for communication, for wisdom, for forgiveness, to forgive, to comfort, whatever the need at the moment, we are doing something concretely *real*. We actually change that reality, creating a different ripple or wave, which then changes our present. When we learn and grow where we are, that change too ripples and waves out to change those other explorations that we have made which interact throughout our entire being. When you enter a past life, then, enter with the idea that you have the power to heal yourself, to clear and clean your pool.

There are many methods that can lead us into awareness of our other explorations. Sometimes dreams are the doorway to the past. Sometimes events will catapult us into awareness of other realities, much like the automobile accident that so affected Sandy's son, Steven. Altered states of conscious such as meditation, day-dreaming, or pre-or post-sleep states often give us glimpses into these others parts of ourselves. Formal hypnosis with a practitioner can be extremely effective, because the practitioner can help you maintain conscious awareness while in the altered state and also can help direct the healing process.

If you find that you are being influenced by the thoughts and feelings of others, then you want to learn how to discriminate between your own thoughts and feelings and theirs. Awareness is always the first step. Pay close attention to your own thoughts and to changes in your mood. Notice what is happening around you, particularly the attitudes and moods of those with whom you live, work, and are emotionally involved. Choose some kind of thought form, which, for you, means psychic protection. Sandy and Sheila choose to visualize themselves surrounded by white light as their protection since white light can act as a filter, allowing in positive and loving thoughts and feelings, deflecting negativity or manipulation. They imbue the thought form—the image of white light—with the intention that it will act as a discriminatory screen. It gives them information about what is happening around them, but also grants the choice to accept others' thoughts and feelings or not. This kind of "protection" is important, particularly for empathic people who often think that the "problem" is always theirs. You may be feeling that you are not "good enough" or that you are always a "bitch" or "depressed" or whatever. Be suspicious when the other or others around you tend to put all the blame for what is happening on you. They may do this directly by telling you that you are such and such a way; or they may imply it by insisting that they are "fine" or "perfect" or "never angry" or "always happy." Reality is always co-created and when one person is thinking all the negative thoughts and feeling all the negative emotions in a relationship, perhaps even acting them out; then it is time to look at what is actually happening. As you learn to separate yourself from the thoughts and feelings of others, you begin to see more clearly what the situation really is. Then you have choice.

Again, it matters little whether you use white light or pink light or some other kind of thought form. What matters is that you become aware that it is important to protect yourself. Choose some kind of thought form, imbuing it with your intention. Some people build walls but walls keep everything out. Choose carefully then. You want all the good stuff coming your way.

When you are in a relationship that has deep bonds and you find that there is a need for separation and balancing, then you may want to investigate the nature of those bonds and clear them out, cutting them on psychic levels for clarity on the physical plane. A technique that Sandy uses frequently and has been referred to several times throughout this book, makes use of "chakras" or energy centers on the auric body. These energy centers contain information about various learning levels that we humans move through as we grow and expand in awareness of our nature. When we are relating to others, there is often interaction on these levels. Perceiving how that interaction takes place can bring clarity to an otherwise murky situation.

Imagine the other person out and away from you about ten feet. You may "see" an image of the person in your mind, or you may "feel" him or her there, or you may simply "think" them there. It does not matter how you do it. There is no right or wrong way. Each person's mind works differently and you need to allow your own mind to communicate with you in its own way.

Next send out a beam of light from you to the other person at each of the following "centers." Once the light is sent out, then passively watch what happens. You may see colors, a direction to the flow of the light, the size and intensity of the light, images that arise, memories, even symbols. You may also feel emotions and/or physical reactions at the various centers. You may "sense" or "know" what is going on at that particular center. Thoughts or insights about the relationship may occur to you as you concentrate. It is most important to trust the communication from your own various levels of consciousness. Some information will come from the unconscious where your memories are stored. Some will come from the higher self where your insight and wisdom originate. Sometimes even the conscious mind will recognize something that it "knew all along."

The first center or "chakra" you want to connect is the earth center. It is located at the perineum, and so if you send light from high between your legs to high between the other's legs and concentrate there, you will begin to receive information about the nature of your relationship in terms of "earth energy." This is the energy of survival, of being in a physical body on the earth plane. It is here that we feel our fear of death. In a relationship, any survival issues that may be occurring will become evident. In a parent/child relationship, this center is naturally an important one and often shows up vividly, either visually or emotionally. It can be important, however, in any relationship.

The second chakra to connect is the sexual center. This is located around the area of the navel. This is where we learn about sensuality and sexuality. In a relationship, any sexual issues will become apparent. It is also where we work out our learning through addictive behaviors, whether that addiction be to a substance or a person. Here you learn the nature of your relationship in terms of this sexual energy.

The third connection should be made at the solar plexus, high in the abdomen where the rib cage makes an upside down V. This is the power chakra. Here we learn about our power and how to assert our will in the world. In our relationships, if manipulating or power struggles are occurring, you will perceive that here. An example of this can be seen in struggles between parents and teenagers. The teenager is often trying very hard to separate from the parent in order to find his or her own identity in the world. The parent wants what he or she feels is best for the child. On the physical plane, all kinds of struggles ensue. By becoming aware of the energy flow on the psychic level, the child can "protect" himself by cutting the connection; or the parent can cut the connection, letting the child go. By doing this psychically, often the parent then knows intuitively what actions to take on the physical plane in order to help the child grow and learn safely. This is only one example of the kinds of power struggles that people create in their relationships.

When another wants you to be a certain way for them and spends time developing and implementing behaviors to accomplish that end, then you may feel that as pressure at the solar plexus. You are being manipulated. The power chakra is where you can learn of these influences.

The fourth connection is the heart chakra. This is the center of emotions and feelings. Here is where we learn acceptance. The heart chakra is one of the most important in terms of our psychological and spiritual growth. In a relationship, you will perceive the effects of emotional energy as it flows between you and another person.

The fifth connection is at the throat. This is the center of self-expression and where we learn to express our creativity in the world. Here you learn the nature of your relationship with the other person in terms of the flow of communication between you. If your communicating is stuck or you each "miss" the other, it will be evident here.

The sixth chakra is at the forehead. This is the psychic center or "third eye" as it is known in occult literature. Here is where you learn the nature of your relationship with the other person in terms of psychic or telepathic energy. Often people are quite surprised at the intensity of this energy. When we are open to others, the flow of their thoughts can easily enter our consciousness. This center, of course, is extremely important in terms of the kinds of influences discussed in this book. Being aware of its existence and how it works in your relationships can give you more choice in how you relate to the other.

The seventh and final center that we use is the "crown" chakra. It usually arches from the top of your head to the top of the other person's head. This is where you learn about your spiritual connection with the other person. You will notice that we have moved from the earth to the "heavens." The connection at the spiritual center may offer you glimpses into past-life interactions. You may also have a strong sense of the depth of the bond that exists between you.

Once you have connected all the seven energy centers, allow your consciousness to move away from yourself a bit to perceive all the connections at once. This perspective gives you an overview of the entire relationship. You will see or sense which connections are strongest, which are weakest, which are positively influencing you and which may be limiting you in some way.

Next, it is now time to clear out all the connections. This is done in order to create a condition of psychic clarity between you and the other person. It matters not whether the connections are viewed as "good" or "bad." Most relationships have some of both. The important point, here, is to introduce clarity. Imagine a white "cleansing" light coming down from the universe. Sandy usually suggests to her clients that they imagine the "Ajax white tornado" from the commercial on television. The idea, of course, is to have some kind of symbol that means "cleaning" or "clearing." Have this cleansing light move through each connection, starting at the crown, moving down through the connection at the forehead, then the one at the throat, next the heart, the solar plexus, the sexual, and finally the earth connection. You should finish with seven clear beams of white light between you and the other. All influences and "information" will be pushed down with the light, to eventually go out through your feet and through the feet of the other person, into the earth. Think of the earth as a "transformer." Ask it to receive your emotional and psychic energy and transform it into something positive and loving, just as it does with our organic physical garbage which becomes new trees, flowers, or vegetables.

The final step is to cut these bonds. This too is done not to send people away on the physical plane, but to create "psychic" space. When people ask for "space" in relationships, they are not usually asking for physical place. They understand that they are feeling pushed or pressured in some way and are, therefore, asking for psychic space. This "cutting" is a way of creating that psychic space in relationships for yourself or for the other person. Choose a cutting instrument—a knife, a scissor, a guillotine, anything that comes to mind—then cut all the beams of white light. Pull your half of the light into your being. Imagine the other person's half of the light entering his or her being. Then surround yourself with a white light (or whatever psychic protection you use). If you like, surround the other person with the same protection but then see that person move far away from you in your inner space. Make sure that there is plenty of "space" between the two of you. Make it real with your imagination. See it, feel it, or think it.

You will be surprised to find shifts or differences in the relationship. Perhaps a "relief." Sometimes you will find that you feel stronger. Or you may find that you suddenly "know" what is going on in the relationship. Sometimes the other person will react with a behavioral change, or even protestation, if he or she has been benefiting by the "contract" you have had together. You may want to do this exercise more than once with a person or periodically with people in your life. Sandy still does this exercise with her son, Griffin, in order to get herself out of his struggles. Remember, it does not mean that you do not love the other person or want the other person in your life. You are asking for psychic clarity and understanding. You are giving yourself and the other person some "breathing room."

You may also find that you can send telepathic messages to the other person that can effect a communication unavailable to you on the physical plane. This is certainly true when you do this process with those who have left the earth plane. Relationships continues even after death. If there is a need for communication with those who have left, this process can set the conditions for that to occur.

As we have seen throughout this book, relationships are "learning grounds" in this physical reality. We work out our various beliefs and patterns together, experimenting constantly with the tools and rules of our "playground," Mother Earth. Sandy and Sheila were greatly influenced in their lives, their relationships, and their work by Jane Roberts and Seth; and so Sandy felt it appropriate to end this book with a lengthly quote from Seth, offering his assessment of the possibilities in relationships between humans:

"Some people are naturally solitary. They want to live lone lives, and are content. Most, however, have a need for enduring close relationships. These provide both a psychic and social framework for personal growth, understanding, and development. It is an easy enough matter to shout to the skies: 'I love my fellow men,' when on the other hand you form no strong, enduring relationship with others. It is easy to claim an equal love for all members of the species, but love itself requires an understanding that at your level of activity is based upon intimate experience. You cannot love someone you do not know, not unless you water down the definition of love so much that it becomes meaningless.

"To love someone, you must appreciate how that person differs from yourself and from others. You must hold that person in mind so that to some extent love is a kind of meditation, a loving focus upon another individual. Once you experience that kind of love, you can translate it into other terms. The love itself spreads out, expands,so that you can then see others in love's light.

"Love is naturally creative and explorative, that is, you want to explore creatively aspects of the beloved one. Even characteristics that would otherwise appear as faults attain a certain loving significance. They are seen and accepted, and yet they make no difference. Because these are still attributes of the beloved one, even the seeming faults are redeemed. The beloved attains prominence over all others.

"The span of God's love can perhaps equally hold within its vision the existences of all individuals at one time in an infinite loving glance that beholds each person, seeing each with all his or her peculiar characteristics and tendencies. Such a God's glance would delight in each person's difference from each other person. This would not be a blanket love, a soupy porridge of a glance in which individuality melted, but a love based on a full understanding of each individual. The emotion of love brings you closest to an understanding of the nature of All That Is. Love incites dedication and commitment. It specifies. You cannot, therefore, honestly insist that you love humanity and all people equally if you do not love one other person. If you do not love yourself, it is quite difficult to love another." (*The Nature of the Psyche: Its Human Expression,* pp. 91-92.)

And so our ultimate goal is to "clear our pool" and learn to love ourselves and then one another. As the murkiness settles and the ripples and waves calm, we begin to live more and more in the wonderfully creative awareness that we are indeed All That Is, experiencing the spreading of a love that we ourselves have generated.

To Reach the Author contact:

Mind Matters
Sandra Stevens
P.O. Box 155, River Road
Washington Crossing, PA. 18977